CONTENTS

THE PONY CLUB TETRATHLON OBJECTIVES

The aim of Pony Club Tetrathlon is to provide Members with a challenging competition requiring sound practical horsemanship and general athletic ability. Competitions include a shoot, swim, run and ride phase, aimed at encouraging competitors to combine their interest in riding and the horse generally with additional skills and athletic challenges, thereby enhancing the enjoyment they derive from The Pony Club.

The rules are relevant to ALL Pony Club Tetrathlon Competitions including Championship, Area, Senior International, Junior International, and Winter Triathlon Competitions. Rules for Arena Jumping, the Winter Triathlon competition and the Stepping Stones competition are contained in the Appendices.

Every eventuality cannot be provided for in these rules. Unforeseen circumstances or issues will be addressed by the relevant Officials in a sporting spirit, and in accordance with the intention of these Rules. It is the competitor's responsibility to ensure that they comply with the Rules of the competition.

RULES

All Rules are made by the Pony Club Tetrathlon Committee in conjunction with other Pony Club Committees.

The Pony Club Office provides administrative support. Queries relating to these rules must be directed to the Tetrathlon Chairman at tetchairman@pcuk.org and copied to the Office at tetrathlon@pcuk.org.

NOTE: Passages that differ from the text of the 2024 edition are printed in bold and side-lined (as this note).

THE PONY CLUB TETRATHLON COMMITTEE

Chairman

▸ Mandy Donaldson
  Email: tetchairman@pcuk.org

Members

▸ Jayne Bowman
▸ Jane Speakman
▸ Heather Williams
▸ Heather Greenslade
▸ Judy Hardcastle
▸ Zoe Kennerley
▸ Alex Connors
▸ Louly Thornycroft (Area Representative)
▸ Susan Goodridge (Area Representative)
▸ Liz Wilkinson (Co-ordinator Chairman)
▸ Richard Mosley (Co-ordinator Representative)

Sports Officer: tetrathlon@pcuk.org

Health and Safety: safety@pcuk.org

PART 1 – GENERAL PONY CLUB TETRATHLON RULES

1.   COMPETITION AGE LIMITS

Pony Club Tetrathlon consists of the following competitions, some of which have varying age requirements. Boys and Girls compete in separate classes unless otherwise stated.

a.   Open Team Competition

Open to all Members aged 25 or under (on 1st January of the current calendar year). Open to Teams of four or three boys or girls, as appropriate, from Branches/Centres. If a team consists of four, then its score is the sum of the best three performances overall.

Any Branch/Centre may enter more than one team.

b.   The Open Individual Competition

Open to all Members aged 25 or under (on 1st January of the current calendar year). The scores for all competitors automatically count for this competition. Branches or Centres may enter Individuals irrespective of whether they have entered a team or not.

c.   Intermediate Team Competition

Open to all Members aged 25 or under (on 1st January of the current calendar year). Teams of four or three boys or girls, as appropriate, from Branches/Centres. If a team consists of four, then its score is the sum of the best three performances overall. Any Branch/Centre may enter more than one team.

d.   The Intermediate Individual Competition

Open to all Members aged 25 or under (on 1st January of the current calendar year). The scores for all competitors automatically count for this competition. Branches or Centres may enter Individuals irrespective of whether they have entered a team or not.

e.   Junior Team Competition

Open to Members aged 14 or under (on 1st January of the current calendar year). Teams of four or three boys or girls, as appropriate, from Branches/Centres. If a team consists of four, then its score is the sum of the best three performances overall. Any Branch/Centre may enter more than one team.

f.   The Junior Individual Competition

Open to Members up to the age of 14 (Ages are taken on 1st January in the current calendar year). The scores for all competitors automatically count for this competition. Branches or Centres may enter Individuals irrespective of whether they have entered a team or not.

g.   Tetrathlon Competition Levels

Competition levels appropriate for Championship qualifiers:

QUALIFYING COMPETITION LEVELS	RIDE	SHOOT	SWIM	RUN
OPEN BOYS (25 and under)	1.00m*	10m Turning Targets One Handed	4 minutes	3000m
OPEN GIRLS (25 and under)	1.00m*	10m Turning Targets One Handed	3 minutes	1500m
INTERMEDIATE BOYS (25 and under)	1.00m	10m Turning Targets One Handed	3 minutes	2000m
INTERMEDIATE GIRLS (25 and under)	1.00m	10m Turning Targets One Handed	3 minutes	1500m
JUNIOR BOYS AND GIRLS (14 and under)	0.90m	7m Turning Targets One Handed	3 minutes	1500m

* At the Tetrathlon Championships, the Open riding competition will increase height to 1.05cm.

g.   Introductory Competitions for Younger or Novice Members

Branches and Centres are encouraged to run events to introduce young and novice Members to Tetrathlon. No person under the age of 8 (on the day of competition) may shoot at a Pony Club event, including postal pistol shoots. The levels of competition defined in the Table on page 9 should be used as a guide. Ages are taken on the 1st January in the current calendar year. Minimus – For Members aged 11 and under Tadpoles – For Members aged 9 and under Beanies – For Members aged 7 and under.

Optional Competition levels that do not qualify for Championships:

NON QUALIFYING COMPETITIONS	RIDE	SHOOT	SWIM	RUN
INTERMEDIATE NOVICE BOYS (25 and under)	0.90m	10m Turning Targets One Handed	3 minutes	2000m
INTERMEDIATE NOVICE GIRLS (25 and under)	0.90m	10m Turning Targets One Handed	3 minutes	1500m
JUNIOR NOVICE BOYS AND GIRLS (14 and under)	0.80m	7m Turning Targets One Handed	3 minutes	1500m
MINIMUS BOYS AND GIRLS (11 and under)	0.80m	7m Turning Targets Two Handed	2 minutes	1000m
MINIMUS NOVICE BOYS AND GIRLS (11 and Under)	0.70m	7m Static Targets Two Handed	2 minutes	1000m
TADPOLES BOYS AND GIRLS (9 and under)	0.60m	7m Static Targets Two Handed	2 minutes	1000m
BEANIES BOYS AND GIRLS (7 and under)	0.40m	Beanbag at target – minimum 3m throw	2 minutes	500m

2.   ORDER OF COMPETITION

The order for completing the four phases (Ride, Run, Shoot and Swim) will be at the discretion of the Organiser. The competition can be completed in one or more days.. An Arena Jumping event may substituted for any non-qualifying classes for all or part of the Ride phase and scoring will be in accordance with Appendix C.

3.   OVERALL SCORE

Competitors score points according to their performance in each phase.

In the Run and Swim phases, scores are based on a standard level of performance for 1000 points, with marks added or deducted according to performance against the standard. In the Shoot, positive marks are awarded for shots on target. The aim is that each phase should have equal influence on the final result. The Ride is scored at 1400 points, less deductions for penalties accumulated. Other than at Area, International and Championship competitions competitors may opt to drop to the next Ride course down, incurring 500 penalties, or alternatively organisers may wish to stage a separate class with a smaller Ride course for more novice competitors.

The scores of a competitor in each of the four phases are added together to give the overall score for the competition. To earn an overall score a competitor must start each phase and must continue until they complete the phase, retire or are disqualified.

4.   TIES

In the event of equality of final scores, the points in the Ride phase shall decide the final placing. If these are the same, the result shall be declared a tie. In the event of a tie for a Challenge Trophy, it shall be held for an equal period by each party concerned. In the case of a tie when qualifying for Championships, all parties concerned shall qualify.

5.   DRESS

The competitor is responsible for complying with all Rules relating to dress for the particular phase of Tetrathlon in which they are participating. Unless otherwise stated, Ride dress is to be worn for prize giving.

6.   SUSPENSION FROM COMPETING FOR MEDICAL REASONS

a.   If a Member is banned/suspended from competing in any sport for medical reasons, they should not compete at any Pony Club event until passed fit for the sport in which they are banned/suspended. It is the responsibility of the Member and parent/guardian to ensure adherence to this rule.

b.   Inhalers – The Doctors on the Safety & Welfare Advisory Committee advise that the use of inhalers whilst running or swimming is dangerous and therefore prohibited. Inhalers may be used before, but not during each phase. If any competitor is so short of breath during a phase that they need an inhaler, then they are not fit to continue and should be stopped.

7.   UNSEEMLY BEHAVIOUR

Unseemly behaviour on the part of competitors, parents, team officials, or team supporters will be reported as soon as possible by the Official Steward to The Pony Club Office. Offenders may be penalised by disqualification of the Branch(es)/Centre(s) concerned for a period up to three years. Should a competitor, or supporter of a competitor, in the opinion of the Official Steward, be rude or aggressive towards any official at the competition, or behave in an aggressive or unfair manner to their horse, the Official Steward may disqualify that competitor.

8.   PERFORMANCE–ENHANCING DRUGS

All performance-enhancing drugs are strictly forbidden and The Pony Club supports 100% clean sport.

a. Equine – Controlled Medication

It is essential for the welfare of a horse/pony that appropriate veterinary treatment is given if and when required. Some medication, however, may mask an underlying health problem so horses and ponies should not take part in training or competition when taking such medication and any Therapeutic Use Exemptions (TUE) should be confirmed in writing by a Vet.

For more information, please refer to the Welfare of Horses and Ponies at Pony Club Activities Policy, available on The Pony Club website.

b. Human

Performance-enhancing drugs are forbidden. The Pony Club supports the approach taken by the UK Anti-Doping Agency in providing clean sport. The Pony Club disciplinary procedures will be used where doping is suspected including reporting to the UK Anti-Doping Agency.

c. Testing

All competitors should be aware that random samples may be taken for testing from both themselves and/or their horse/pony. The protocol used will be that of the relevant adult discipline.

Competitors and their horses/ponies at national or international level may be subject to blood tests in line with the Sports Council Policy on illegal and prescribed substances. All young people competing at these levels should be aware of this.

d. Reporting

i. Anyone who has reasonable grounds for suspecting that a Member is using or selling an illegal substance must report their concerns to the District Commissioner/Centre Proprietor as soon as practicable. If there is an immediate risk to the health, safety or welfare of one or more Members then the Police must be informed as soon as possible. The person reporting their concerns must ensure that any material evidence is retained

ii. Upon receiving a report of suspected use or selling of an illegal substance, the District Commissioner/Centre Proprietor should carry out an immediate investigation of the incident and the circumstances in which it occurred, and then decide upon the appropriate action to be taken. This will include:

- Informing the Member's parents/guardians
- Informing The Pony Club Area Representative who in turn will inform The Pony Club Office
- Informing the Police
- Suspending the Member concerned while investigations are completed
- Awaiting the completion of Police investigations and actions

Disciplinary Action

The normal disciplinary procedure should be followed in cases relating to alcohol or drugs, which can be found in The Pony Club Handbook.

9.   DISQUALIFICATION

The Official Steward may disqualify a competitor at any stage of the competition:

a.   for dangerous riding

b.   if, their opinion, the horse is lame, sick or exhausted

c.   for misuse of whip, spur or bit, or ill–treatment of the horse

d.   for any breach of the rules

e.   for unseemly behaviour, including bad language.

When there is no Official Steward the District Commissioner or the Organiser acts in their place. A competitor who is disqualified at any stage of the competition scores nought for the whole competition and takes no further part in it.

10.   STEWARDS, OFFICIALS AND JUDGES

a.   Official Steward

The Pony Club Tetrathlon Committee shall appoint an Official Steward for each Area Competition. Their duties are as follows:

i.   They are responsible for inspecting the courses and arrangements for all phases before these are shown to the competitors. They are authorised to insist on alterations if they are not in all respects within the limits laid down in the Rules or, in their opinion, are unsuitable for competition.

ii.   They will be present on the days of the Tetrathlon competition to ensure that it is conducted in accordance with the Rules, to take part in the briefing of the Judges, to act as Chairman of the Jury of Appeal and to give help and guidance as may be required.

iii.   They should check that the Medical, Veterinary and First Aid arrangements for the riding phase are in accordance with Tetrathlon Rules and The Pony Club Health and Safety Rule Book.

iv.   They may not be called upon to undertake any other duties at Tetrathlon competitions.

v.   They are authorised to disqualify individuals or a team for misconduct.

b.   At other Tetrathlon competitions, the Organiser shall be responsible for ensuring that these duties are carried out and in particular that the riding course is inspected by an experienced person approved by the Area Representative or Tetrathlon Coordinator.

c.   Phase Stewards and Judges

These will be appointed by the competition Organiser. All should be briefed by the Organiser/Official Steward as to their duties and responsibilities during the competition.

11.   JURY OF APPEAL

All Members of the Jury of Appeal must remain at the competition venue for half an hour after the scores have been published.

The Jury of Appeal will consist of the Organiser, the Steward of the phase concerned and the Official Steward, who should act as Chairman, and will have a casting vote.

The Official Steward may appoint a replacement for any Member of the Jury if the need arises.

The Championship Jury of Appeal is to consist of:

a. The Chairman of Tetrathlon

b. The Steward of the Phase concerned

c. Any Member of the Tetrathlon Committee present.

12.   PROTESTS OR OBJECTIONS

Apart from the Official Steward, Officials of the competition and the Area Representative, only District Commissioners/Centre Proprietors or their appointed Representatives are entitled to lodge objections or protests. Protests must be made in writing and addressed to the Organiser of the competition or Secretary of the Championships. The originator of a protest may amplify his case before the Jury of Appeal, but will not be present at their deliberations. Protests must be accompanied by a deposit of £50 which is forfeited unless the Jury of Appeal decides that there were good and reasonable grounds for the objection. Protests must be made within half an hour of the incident occurring, or within half an hour of publication of the scores. The Jury of Appeal will give their decision after investigation and their decision is final.

The procedures defined above apply to formal protests only. Requests for information may be made to the Organiser at any convenient time.

13.   SPONSORSHIP

In the case of competitors and horses, no form of advertising, including a sponsor's name, may appear on the competitor's or horse's clothing and equipment at a Pony Club competition. The wearing of clothing for horses or riders that has been presented by sponsors of the Championships in the current or previous years is allowed. Sponsors at Area Competitions must not be business competitors of the main sponsors of the sport, and must be approved by The Pony Club Office. Any advertising material that is used by sponsors, whether it be in the form of display banners or programme material, must be tasteful, and appropriate to the image of The Pony Club.

14.   INSURANCE

The Pony Club 'Public and Products Liability Insurance' Policy includes cover for all the official Area Competitions and the Championships. Details of this insurance are available on The Pony Club website.

In the event of any accident, loss or damage occurring to a third party or to the property of a third party (including the general public and competitors) no liability should be admitted, and full details should be sent at once to The Pony Club Office.

The following statements should be included in all event schedules:

HEALTH AND SAFETY

Organisers of events take reasonable precautions to ensure the Health and Safety of everyone present. For these measures to be effective, everyone must take all reasonable precautions to avoid and prevent accidents occurring and must obey the instructions of the organisers and all the officials and stewards.

LEGAL LIABILITY

Save for the death or personal injury caused by the negligence of the organisers, or anyone for whom they are in law responsible, neither the organisers of this event or The Pony Club nor any agent, employee or representative of these bodies, nor the landlord or their tenant, accepts any liability for any accident, loss, damage, injury or illness to horses, owners, riders, spectators, land, cars, their contents and accessories, or any other person or property whatsoever. Entries are only accepted on this basis.

15.   MEDICAL COVER

Medical cover required at each phase of a Pony Club Tetrathlon Competition is detailed in The Pony Club Health, Safety, Safeguarding and Horse Welfare Rulebook.

PART 2 – THE INDIVIDUAL PHASE RULES

RIDING – RULES

16.   HORSE ELIGIBILITY

a.   There is no height limit.

b.   No horse/pony under 5 years of age is eligible. A horse or pony shall be deemed to reach the age of 1 on the 1st January following the date on which it is foaled and shall be deemed to become a year older on each successive 1st January.

c.   At Area competitions and the Championships a horse may be shared by two Members of the same family (i.e. by a brother and sister, two brothers or two sisters). At less formal competitions the Organiser may allow a horse to be shared by no more than two competitors. A horse running for the second time at The Championships must be passed by the vet as being fit to compete. The ultimate responsibility for a horse that has been passed by the vet to run for a second time lies with the parent/owner.

d.   Horses that are graded British Eventing Advanced (Grade 1) and have competed at OI/AI/A level during the current calendar year are not eligible at any level.

e.   Stallions can be ridden by Members only if they obtain written permission from their District Commissioner. They must wear identifying discs on their bridle in the interests of safety

17.   DRESS AND EQUIPMENT

Equipment must be clean, neat, tidy and safe.

It is the competitor's responsibility to ensure their dress complies with the Rules. Contravention may incur disqualification. Apart from Cross Country colours and silks, brightly coloured accessories must not be worn.

a.   Hat and Hair Rule

Hair: Must be tied up and back (preferably in a hairnet) and securely, in a safe manner to reduce the risk of hair being caught and to prevent scalp injuries.

Hats: Members must always wear a protective hat when mounted. Only hats to the following specifications are acceptable at any Pony Club activity. The Pony Club is consistent with fellow BEF (British Equestrian) Member bodies in its Standards for Riding Hats. Individual sports may have additional requirements with regard to colour and type. It is strongly recommended that secondhand hats are not purchased.

The hat standards accepted as of 1st January 2025 are detailed in the table below:

Hat Standard	Safety Mark
Snell E2016 & 2021 with the official Snell label and number	
PAS 015: 2011 with BSI Kitemark or Inspec IC Mark	
(BS) EN 1384:2023 with BSI Kitemark or Inspec IC Mark	
VG1 with BSI Kitemark or Inspec IC Mark	
ASTM-F1163 2015 & 2023 with the SEI mark	
AS/NZS 3838, 2006 with SAI Global Mark	

Note: Some hats are dual-badged with different standards. If a hat contains at least one compliant hat standard it is deemed suitable to competition, even if it is additionally labelled with an older standard.

▸ For cross-country (at all levels) riding including Eventing, Arena Eventing, Tetrathlon and Hunter Trials, together with Pony Racing (whether it be tests, rallies, competition or training) and Mounted Games competitions, a jockey skull cap must be worn with no fixed peak, peak type extensions or noticeable protuberances above the eyes or to the front, and should have an even round or elliptical shape with a smooth or slightly abrasive surface, having no peak or peak type extensions. Noticeable protuberances above the eyes or to the front not greater than 5mm, smooth and rounded in nature are permitted. A removable hat cover with a light flexible peak may be used if required.

- ▶ No recording device is permitted (e.g. hat cameras) as they may have a negative effect on the performance of the hat in the event of a fall.

- ▶ The fit of the hat and the adjustment of the harness are as crucial as the quality. Members are advised to try several makes to find the best fit. The hat should not move on the head when the head is tipped forward. The Pony Club recommends you visit a qualified BETA (British Equestrian Trade Association) fitter.

- ▶ Hats must be replaced after a severe impact as subsequent protection will be significantly reduced. Hats deteriorate with age and should be replaced after three to five years depending upon the amount of use.

- ▶ Hats must be worn at all times (including at prize-giving) when mounted with a chinstrap fastened and adjusted so as to prevent movement of the hat in the event of a fall.

- ▶ For Show Jumping: hat covers, if applicable, shall be dark blue, black or brown only. Branch/Centre team colours are permitted for team competitions.

- ▶ The Official Steward/Organiser may, at their discretion, eliminate a competitor riding in the area of the competition without a hat or with the chinstrap unfastened or with a hat that does not comply with these standards.

Hat Checks and Tagging

The Pony Club and its Branches and Centres will appoint Officials, who are familiar with The Pony Club hat rule, to carry out hat checks and tag each hat that complies with the requirements set out in the hat rule with an Pony Club hat tag. Hats fitted with a Pony Club, British Eventing (BE) or British Riding Club (BRC) hat tag will not need to be checked on subsequent occasions. However, the Pony Club reserves the right to randomly spot check any hat regardless of whether it is already tagged.

Tagging is an external verification of the internal label and indicates that a hat meets the accepted standards. The tag does NOT imply any check of the fit and condition of the hat has been undertaken. It is considered to be the responsibility of the Member's parent(s) / guardian(s) to ensure that their hat complies with the required standards and is tagged before they go to any Pony Club event. Also, they are responsible for ensuring that the manufacturer's guidelines with regard to fit and replacement are followed.

For further information on hat standards, testing and fitting, please refer to the British Equestrian Trade Association (BETA) website: British Equestrian Trade Association - Safety and your head (beta-uk.org)

b.   **Jackets –** Riders may wear either a hacking jacket (worn with shirt and Pony Club tie or hunting stock) or Cross Country colours. A self –tied stock is recommended. A Pony Club Stock with any jacket is permitted. As a minimum shoulders must be covered while competing. Jackets may be removed during riding in, provided that the competitor is wearing a shirt with sleeves. Numbers should be worn at all times.

c.   **Gloves –** Gloves are optional for cross country

d.   **Breeches –** white, cream, beige, dark or muted colours may be worn. Dark-coloured contrast seats are permitted.

e.   **Footwear –** Only standard riding or jodhpur boots with a well-defined square cut heel may be worn. Plain black or brown half chaps may be worn with jodhpur boots of the same colour. Tassels and fringes are not allowed. No other footwear will be permitted, including wellington boots, yard boots, country boots, "muckers" or trainers. Boots with interlocking treads are not permitted, nor are the boots or treads individually.

Stirrups should be of the correct size to suit the rider's boots (see the Stirrup rule). Laces on boots must be taped for Mounted Games only.

f.   **Spurs – may not be worn by a Pony Club member at a Pony Club activity or event unless that member has passed either the Pony Club C+ Riding Test or the Pony Club Spurs Test.** Any misuse of spurs will be reported to the DC/Centre Proprietor, Area Representative and Training Chairman; any reported riders will be recorded and monitored.

Sharp spurs are not permitted. Only blunt spurs, without rowels or sharp edges, and spurs that have a smooth rotating ball on the shank may be worn. If the spurs are curved, the curve must be downwards, and the shank must point straight to the back. **The Pony Club recommends a spurs length of no greater than 2.5cm - the measurement is taken from the back of the boot to the end of the shank. No spurs with a length greater than 4cm are permitted.**

Spurs must only be used to enhance the normal leg aids and allow for better communication from rider to horse.

Spurs must never be used to vent a competitor's anger or to reprimand the horse.

Use of the spurs which causes injury e.g.. blood, broken skin or a weal, is always classed as misuse.

Misuse of the spurs anywhere at the event will result in disqualification.

g.   Body Protectors – A body protector is compulsory for all Pony Club Cross Country riding (including Arena Eventing) and Pony Racing activities whether it be training or competition. A body protector for these activities must meet BETA 2018 Level 3 Standard (blue and black label).

For general use, the responsibility for choosing body protectors and the decision as to their use must rest with Members and their parents. It is recommended that a rider's body protector should not be more than 2% of their body weight. When worn, body protectors must fit correctly, be comfortable and must not restrict movement. BETA recommends body protectors are replaced at least every three to five years, after which the impact absorption properties of the foam may have started to decline.

Air Jackets

If a rider chooses to wear an air jacket in Cross country or Pony Racing, it must only be used in addition with a normal body protector which meets BETA 2018 Level 3 standard (blue and black label). Parents and Members must be aware that riders may be permitted to continue after a fall in both competitions and training rides for Cross Country and / or Pony Racing if the First Aid provider has no concerns about their welfare. In the event of a fall, an air jacket must be fully deflated or removed before continuing, the conventional body protector must continue to be worn. Air jackets must not be worn under a jacket. Number bibs should be fitted over the air jacket loosely or with elasticised fastenings.

h.   Medical armbands are advised if Members are not accompanied by a responsible adult, including if hacking on roads.

i.   Jewellery – the wearing of any sort of jewellery when handling or riding a horse/pony is not recommended and if done at any Pony Club activity, is done at the risk of the member/their parent/guardian. However, to stop any risk of injury, necklaces and bracelets (other than medical bracelets) must be removed, as must larger and more pendulous pieces of jewellery (including those attached to piercings) which create a risk of injury to the body part through which they are secured. For the avoidance of doubt a wristwatch, wedding ring, stock pin worn horizontally and/or a tie clip are permitted. It is recommended that stock pins are removed for cross country.

j.   **Buttonholes** may not be worn.

k.   **Prize giving –** Competitors must be correctly dressed in their competition riding clothes for prize givings, either mounted or dismounted. Only saddlery that falls within the rules of the competition will be allowed.

l.   **Course Walking –** Whilst course walking competitors must be tidily dressed but not necessarily in riding clothes.

m.   **Whips –** A whip, if carried, must be held in the hand by the handle with the handle at the top. The whip must be "padded".

The maximum length of the "Whip" is 70cm and must be no less than 45cm.

- The "Contact area", is considered to be 2/5's (two fifths) of the overall length of the "Whip" and must be covered with a "Pad".
- There must be no "binding" within 17 centimetres of the end of the "Pad".
- The "Pad" must be smooth, with no protrusion or raised surface, and be made of shock absorbing material throughout its circumference such that it gives a compression factor of at least 6mm.
- There is to be no wording, advertising or personalisation of any kind on the "Pad".

At all times, the whip must only be used

- For a good reason, as an aid to encourage the horse forward or as a reprimand.
- At an appropriate time, namely when the horse is reluctant to go forward under normal aids of seat and legs or as a reprimand immediately after a horse has been disobedient.
- In the right place, namely down the shoulder or behind the leg but never overarm.
- No more than twice for any one incident.

Excessive use of the whip anywhere at the event will result in elimination of the rider from any competition which has already taken place and disqualification of the rider from competing for the rest of the day. The following are always considered excessive and will result in immediate elimination:

- Use of the whip to vent a competitor's anger.
- Use of a whip which causes injury e.g. Broken skin or a weal.

- ► Use after elimination or retirement.
- ► Use on a horse's head, neck etc.
- ► Using the whip from the ground after a rider fall or dismount.
- ► If the rider's arm comes above the shoulder when using the whip.

n. **Electronic devices** (i.e. headphones, mobile phones etc. enabling another person to communicate with the rider) are not allowed while the rider is competing. No recording device is permitted (e.g. head/bridle cameras etc.)

Stopwatches may be worn at Junior Level and above.

18. SADDLERY

It is the Competitor's responsibility to ensure that their tack is in accordance with the rules and that they present themselves for inspection. Any competitor who presents to compete in the wrong saddlery/equipment will not be allowed to compete until they decide to re–present in correct saddlery/equipment. Any competitor who then changes their tack after the tack inspection will be disqualified from the competition.

The Official Steward has the absolute discretion to forbid the use of any bit, gadget, spur or boot which they consider cruel or misused.

Any misuse of a bit/bridle will be reported to the DC/Centre Proprietor, Area Representative and Training Chairman. Any reported riders will be recorded and monitored.

Any equipment not covered in these Rules must be referred at least two weeks in advance of the competition to the Pony Club Office to allow time for the Chairman of Tetrathlon to be consulted. All tack must be correctly fitted. Disabled riders are welcome to apply to The Pony Club Office to use special equipment.

a. **Bridles** – Plain black or brown bridles only may be used. For safety reasons leather bridles are recommended. The Micklem Multibridle is permitted without bit clips.

b. **Nosebands** – Only one may be worn unless using a Standing martingale with a combination, Kineton, drop noseband or similar in which case the addition of a cavesson is allowed. Nosebands must be correctly fitted and should not cause discomfort. Nosebands must not incorporate chain. Sheepskin nosebands are permitted.

c. **Bits** – All synthetic bits must be black, brown or white. Any normal riding bit is accepted, hackamore or any bitless bridle. Bits should be in their original manufactured state.

d.   **Tongue Guards** – are permitted. The use of tongue straps, tongue grids, string, twine or cord in or around the horse's mouth is forbidden.

e.   **Reins** – Split reins, Ernest Dillon reins, Market Harborough and balancing, running, draw, check or bridge reins of any kind are forbidden. (A running, draw or check rein is one which is attached to the saddle, girth, martingale or breast plate on the horse).

Grass and balanced support reins

Grass reins and balanced support reins are permitted at Pony Club rallies and competitions jumping up to 50cm or in the Walk and Trot Test subject to the following.

Only those reins shown in diagrams 1 and 2 (and 5) are permitted.

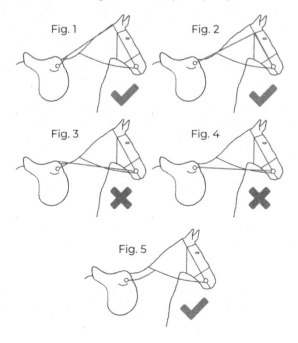

The reins must be fitted to allow and not restrict the normal head position of the pony. The rein length must be sufficient to allow the pony to stretch over a small fence.

Reins may be leather or synthetic material, if synthetic then a break point of leather or other suitable material must be included.

f.   **Neckstraps** may be worn.

g.   **Saddle –** Only black or brown in colour are allowed of plain English type.

h.   **Stirrups** should be of the correct size to suit the rider's boots. They must have 7mm (¼") clearance on either side of the boot. To find this measurement, tack checkers should move the foot across to one side of the stirrup, with the widest part of the foot on the tread. From the side of the boot to the edge of the stirrup should not be less than 14mm.

There are now many types of stirrups marketed as 'safety stirrups'. All riders must ensure that their stirrups are suitable for the type of footwear they are wearing and the activities in which they are taking part and that the stirrup leathers are in good condition.

There are no prescribed weight limits on metal stirrups, however with the advent of stirrups of other materials, weight limits are frequently given by manufacturers. Any person buying these stirrups, should comply with weight limits defined on the box or attached information leaflets. Neither the feet nor the stirrup leathers or irons, may be attached to the girth, nor the feet attached to the stirrup irons.

It is strongly recommended that the design of the stirrup chosen allows the foot to be released easily in the event of a rider fall. Specific rules for individual sports can be found in the respective sports rulebooks.

Particular focus should be on ensuring that the boot and stirrup are the correct size for the rider taking part and used in line with the manufacturer's guidance.

For the avoidance of doubt, at Pony Club events:

- stirrups which connect the boot and the stirrup magnetically are not allowed
- Interlocking boot soles and stirrup treads are not allowed

i.   **Saddle Cloths/Numnahs –** Any solid colour is permitted. Contrasting piping is permitted. Branch logos are allowed when competing for the Branch; logos must not exceed 200 sq. cm. This does not preclude the wearing of clothing for horses or riders that has been presented by sponsors of the Championships in the current or previous years.

j.   **Martingales –** The only martingales permitted are Irish, Standing, Running or Bib, only one of which may be worn at the same time. Standing martingales may be attached only to a plain cavesson noseband which is fitted above the bit.

k. **Girths –** Humane girths pose an increased risk as many common designs may have complete girth failure if a single strap was to break. Humane girths are not permitted in any Sport, whether during training or competition.

Humane Girths have non-independent straps that will loosen should one of the straps break.

l. **Blinkers, leather cheek pieces** or any attachment to the horse/pony or bridle, which may affect the animal's field of vision are prohibited. Sheepskin may be used on the bridle providing the sheepskin does not exceed 3cm in diameter measured from the animal's face.

m. **Bit guards** made entirely of rubber and smooth on both sides are permitted.

n. Competitors using Saddlery and Gadgets on the day of the Riding phase which are not allowed in the competition will be eliminated. Lungeing in side reins, but not bearing, check or balancing reins, is permitted. Side reins must be attached under the saddle flaps and NOT passed between the forelegs.

o. **Hoof Boots –** will not be permitted.

p. **Fly hoods, nose nets and ear covers –** are permitted for all competitions. The ear cover/fly fringe must not cover the horse's eyes.

Ear plugs are not permitted and spot checks may be carried out. Nose nets are permitted. Nose nets must cover the nose only leaving the mouth and bit visible.

19.   ACTION AFTER A FALL/INJURY

A rider who falls and wishes to remount to continue around the course must be examined by the appointed paramedic or doctor before continuing. Should the paramedic or doctor have any concerns regarding the rider's fitness to continue, the rider must retire. Every fall must be recorded onto a signed and dated document and must include the time, date, decision, findings and justification of the decision made. A rider who is permitted to remount and continue should have the time that has elapsed between the fall and the re-start deducted from his overall time. A rider who decides to retire after a fall must be examined by the appointed medical personnel before competing in the next phase of competition or traveling home. It is recommended that riders that remounted be checked again before they travel home.

a) Head injury and concussion

If a person is diagnosed with a concussion, they must not ride or take part in any Pony Club organised activity that involves close contact/handling or riding of horses or ponies for 21 days. This may need to be extended if symptoms persist, on the advice of the treating doctor. All concussion must be reported to Head Office using the online accident report form or by email if it occurred outside of The Pony Club. Concussion advice should be followed without exception.

Head injuries and concussion can be very serious and life changing. Serious head injuries are usually obvious, but concussion can be very subtle. It may not be immediately apparent but should be taken very seriously. Recovery from concussion should be managed carefully.

This rule should be read in conjunction with:

► The Pony Club Concussion Advice

► UK Government Concussion Guidelines

Please contact safety@pcuk.org for further support and advice.

Please see Appendix F for the Head Injury and Concussion Flowchart.

20.   DESTRUCTION OF SEVERELY INJURED HORSES

If in the opinion of the Official Veterinary Surgeon a horse ought to be destroyed on humane grounds, the following procedure will apply. If the owner or their authorised representative is present, the Official Veterinary Surgeon will first obtain their agreement. If the owner or their representative is not available, the Official Steward, acting on the advice of the Official Veterinary Surgeon, may order the destruction of a horse.

N.B. Owners should be aware that this Rule is slightly at variance with The Protection of Animals Act 1911 Section 11, which states that, in the absence of the owner, a Police Constable acting on the advice of a registered Veterinary Surgeon may order the destruction of a horse. This Rule is framed to avoid unnecessary suffering to a severely injured horse.

21.   VACCINATION

A valid passport and vaccination record:

► must accompany the horse/pony to all events

- ▸ must be available for inspection by the event officials
- ▸ must be produced on request at any other time during the event

All ponies/horses must be compliant with the current Pony Club minimum vaccination requirements - please see the website for the current rule.

Note: Events that are held at other venues may be subject to additional specific rules. For example, any horse/pony entering a Licensed Racecourse Property must comply with the Vaccination requirements as set by the British Horseracing Authority. Similar restrictions apply in the cases of certain polo venues. If you are intending to compete under FEI Rules you will need to ensure you are compliant with those Rules.

22.   EXERCISE

a.   Competitors may exercise their horses only in the area provided. They must not be exercised in the car park or horsebox park or among spectators. They may not be ridden on, over or near any part of the cross country course.

b.   On the day of the competition, horses competing may be ridden only by their designated riders, or in exceptional circumstances and only with the permission of the Official Steward, by another member of the same team.

c.   Lungeing of a horse is only permitted in areas designated by the organiser who may also prohibit it completely at their discretion. If allowed, lungeing may be carried out by either the rider or other persons. Lungeing of a horse and rider is prohibited.

23.   RAPPING

Rapping at, or anywhere in the vicinity of the event, is strictly prohibited. Rapping is defined as raising, throwing or moving a pole, stick, rope or other object against one or more of the legs of a horse while it is jumping an obstacle so that the horse is induced to raise such leg or legs higher in order to clear the obstacle.

24.   THE CROSS COUNTRY COURSE

a.   The length of the course and number of jumping efforts will vary according to the level, as outlined in the table on page 43. The course will include a slip rail to take down and replace dismounted, and a gate to open and shut mounted. All obstacles must be jumped in numerical order. There shall be at least 3 alternative 'L' Obstacles or black flag alternatives. Each 'L' Obstacle may consist of only one easy element.

b. **Inspection of the course**

i. At all Branch, International, Area and Championship competitions the cross country course must be completed and ready for inspection by competitors, on foot only, by 2.00p.m. on the day preceding the riding phase. The course may be open before this time, but competitors must be aware that alterations may still be made.

ii. Unauthorised alteration to or tampering with obstacles, direction flags, stringing and foliage on the course is strictly forbidden and may be penalised by disqualification.

iii. A plan of the course shall be displayed by the time it is open for inspection. It must include:

- The course to be followed and its length

- The time allowed

- The numbering of the obstacles

- The identification of the gate to be opened and slip rail to be taken down

- Any compulsory turning points

- Any hazards

- Obstacles having 'L' or black line alternatives

c. **Modification of the course**

i. **Before the test starts** – after the course is open for inspection by competitors at 2pm on the day before the cross country test, no alteration may be made, except that, where exceptional circumstances (such as heavy rain) make one or more obstacles unfair or dangerous, the Official Steward is authorised to reduce the severity of or to by–pass such obstacles. In such a case the Chief Steward of the riding phase and every competitor must be officially and personally informed of the alteration before the start of the test. An Official may be stationed at the place where an alteration has been made, in order to warn competitors.

ii. **During the test** – No modification of the obstacles is allowed, but if it is necessary in the interests of safety to order an obstacle to be by–passed during the competition, all jumping faults previously incurred at the obstacle shall be cancelled, except in the case of a competitor who has incurred refusals at that obstacle which result in retirement. A competitor who has retired shall NOT be reinstated in the phase. Once taken out, the obstacle shall NOT be reintroduced.

d.   Marking the course

Boundary Flags – Red or white boundary flags or indicators are used to mark the start and finish and compulsory sections of the course, to define obstacles and to indicate compulsory changes of direction. Flags are to be placed in such a way that the rider must leave a red flag on their right and a white flag on their left. Such red or white flags or indicators are to be respected under penalty of retirement, wherever they occur on the course, whether singly or in pairs. Only obstacles which are numbered and marked by two boundary flags are judged as obstacles. All boundary and turning flags must be in position prior to the course being open for inspection. All fences immediately adjacent to those that are included in the course should be cross flagged to ensure the safety of competitors and spectators.

Direction markers (yellow or orange) are placed so as to mark the route and help the rider in keeping to the course. They may be passed on either side and keeping close to them is not necessary. Boundary flags and direction markers shall be large and placed in conspicuous positions. Compulsory Turning Flags may be used only if absolutely necessary and will have the red flag on the right and the white flag on the left. They should be marked on the plan of the course.

Black Line Flags (a black line on red and white boundary flags) are used to show that an obstacle, either single or made up of several elements, has an alternative route which may be jumped without penalty. Both sets of flags will be marked with a black line. A competitor is permitted to change without penalty from one black line flagged route to another (e.g. jumping 9A left hand route then 9B right hand route) provided they have not presented their horse at the next element of the original line. After having negotiated all other elements, passing around the last element to be jumped will not be penalised.

'L' markers are used to denote an easier alternative to the 'main' obstacle, to help the less experienced to complete the Cross Country phase/ All 'L' obstacles will be marked with red and white boundary flags. **'L' obstacles may be marked either** with a marker having a red 'L' on a white background beneath the fence number, **OR a marker having an 'L' on the same background colour as the markers for that course**. Jumping an 'L' fence incurs 70 penalties.

Where different parts of an obstacle apply to different classes the part to be negotiated by the class competing at the time, and only that part, must be defined by such flags. Alternatives not to be jumped must be clearly marked to that effect, e.g. by crossed flags. Notices must be affixed indicating where flags are to be for the alternative classes.

A numbered fence should use EITHER "Black Line Flags OR "L" markers, not both.

e.   Starting

At Area Competitions and the Championships, competitors must start from within a simple enclosure erected at the start and made of wooden post and wooden or plastic rails measuring approximately 5m square, with an open front marked with a red and a white flag. If this enclosure has an entrance at the side, this must be approximately 2m wide and should be padded or constructed in such a way that neither horse nor rider entering through the side can be injured. At Branch/Centre events red and white boundary flags on their own may be used at the discretion of the Organiser. A competitor may only start when given the signal to do so by the starter. The starter will count down from five before giving the signal to start and the competitor may move around the enclosure as they please. A competitor who starts early will have their time recorded from the moment they start. Deliberately starting early or cantering through the start may incur retirement at the discretion of the Official Steward. If the horse fails to cross the start line within 60 seconds of the signal being given, the competitor shall retire. Assistance within the starting enclosure is permitted, providing it ceases immediately the signal to start is given. From that instant, the competitor is considered to be on the course and any subsequent assistance is forbidden.

f.   Time Keeping

Time is counted from the signal to start until the instant when the horse's nose passes the finishing post. It is counted in whole seconds, fractions being taken to the next second above, e.g. 30.2 seconds is recorded as 31 seconds. When it is necessary for an Official to stop a competitor on the course while an obstacle is being repaired, because of an accident, or because another competitor is negotiating the gate or slip rail, the period during which a competitor is held up will be recorded by the Fence Judge and deducted from their overall time to give their correct time for completing the course.

g.   Speed and Pace

Throughout the event, competitors are free to choose the pace at which they ride. They should, however, always take account of the requirements of each phase, the prevailing conditions and terrain, the fitness and ability of themselves and their horse and all other factors which may be relevant to the welfare of both horse and rider. On the cross country course, they must also have regard to and respect the class speed and the optimum time.

Speed

The time allowed for completing the course is calculated on a speed of 475m per minutes for Open and Intermediate and 450m per minute for Junior Tetrathlon, plus a total of 60 seconds to allow for the gate and slip rail. Minimus courses and below shall not be timed. There is no time limit and ties are not decided by the fastest time nor by proximity to the time allowed.

h.   Penalties

i)   General Course Penalties

▸ **First refusal, run out or circle of horse at obstacle**
  60 penalties
▸ **Second refusal, run out or circle of horse at obstacle**
  100 penalties
▸ **Third refusal, run out or circle of horse at obstacle**
  Retirement
▸ **Jumping or presenting at an Alternative 'L' Obstacle**
  70 penalties
▸ **First fall of rider anywhere on the course**
  90 penalties
▸ **Second fall of rider**
  Retirement
▸ **Fall of horse**
  Retirement
▸ **Error of course not rectified**
  Retirement
▸ **Omission of obstacle or boundary flag**
  Retirement
▸ **Horse trapped in an obstacle**
  Retirement
▸ **Jumping obstacle in wrong order**
  Retirement
▸ **Jumping obstacle in wrong direction**
  Retirement
▸ **Retaking an obstacle already jumped**
  Retirement
▸ **Horse resisting mounted rider anywhere on the course for 60 seconds**

Retirement

▸ **Failure to negotiate a hazard within 60 seconds**
Retirement

▸ **Continuing the course without a hat**
Disqualification

▸ **Every completed second in excess of time allowed**
2 penalties

Gate

▸ **Having passed through the gate, failure to close it from the departure side of the obstacle within 60 seconds. (Timing to commence when the competitor initially touches the gate).**
50 penalties

▸ **Jumping the gate**
60 penalties

▸ **Failure to open and pass through the gate mounted within 60 seconds (Timing to commence when the competitor initially touches the gate).**
200 penalties

▸ **Failure to attempt to pass through and close the gate until successful or for the full period of 60 seconds.**
Retirement

Slip Rail

Timing to commence upon competitor dismounting and to stop when slip rail has been replaced.

▸ **Failure to drop the top rail correctly (the top rail must touch the ground within the spread of the two flagged uprights and may be placed either side of the bottom rail (see diagram opposite)**
50 penalties

▸ **Having correctly passed over the lower rail, failure to replace the upper rail from the departure side of the obstacle within 60 seconds**
50 penalties

▸ **Damage caused to slip rail**
50 penalties

▸ **Receiving assistance to remount after the slip rail**
70 penalties

▸ **Jumping the slip rail**
60 Penalties

▸ **Failure to dismount, correctly take down the upper rail, and get both competitor and pony to the departure side of the lower rail**

within 60 seconds.
200 penalties

▸ **Failure to attempt to pass through and replace the slip rail until successful or for the full period of 60 seconds.**
Retirement

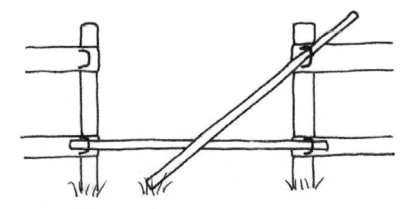

I.   **Definition of faults**

There are no penalty zones. Faults (refusals, run–outs, circling and falls) will be penalised only if, in the opinion of the Judge concerned, they are connected with the negotiation or attempted negotiation of one of the numbered obstacles.

i.   **Refusal – At obstacles or elements with height (i.e. exceeding 30cm)**

A horse is considered to have refused if it stops in front of the obstacle or element to be jumped.

After a refusal, if the competitor redoubles or changes their efforts without success, or if the horse is represented at the obstacle after stepping back and stops or steps back again, this is a second refusal and so on.

ii.   **Refusal – At all other obstacles or elements (i.e. 30cm or less in height)**

A horse is considered to have refused if it stops in front of the obstacle or element to be jumped. A stop followed immediately by a standing jump is not penalised, but if the halt is sustained or in any way prolonged, this constitutes a refusal. The horse may step sideways but if the horse steps back with even one foot, this is a refusal. After a refusal, if the competitor redoubles or changes their efforts without success, or if the horse is represented at the obstacle after stepping back and stops or steps back again, this is a second refusal and so on.

iii. **Run out** – A horse is considered to have run out if it avoids an obstacle to be jumped and runs out to one side or the other. A horse will be considered to have cleared a fence when the head, neck and both shoulders of the horse pass between the extremities of the element or obstacle as flagged.

iv. **Circle** – A horse is considered to have circled if it re–crosses its original track, from whichever direction while negotiating or attempting to negotiate the obstacle, or any part thereof.

If after completing the negotiation of all elements of an obstacle, a horse's exit track from that obstacle crosses its approach track to that obstacle, the horse is not considered to have circled, and will not be penalised.

If a horse completes a circle while being represented at the obstacle after a refusal, run–out or fall, it is only penalised for the refusal, run–out or fall. A competitor may circle without penalty between two separately numbered obstacles even if they are quite close together, provided he clearly does not present the horse in an attempt to negotiate the second obstacle after jumping the first. However, if two or more elements of an obstacle are lettered A, B or C, i.e. are designed as one integral test, then any circling between these elements shall be penalised.

v. **Fall of Rider** – A rider is considered to have fallen when they are separated from their horse in such a way as to necessitate remounting or vaulting into the saddle.

vi. **Fall of Horse** – A horse is considered to have fallen when the shoulder and quarters have touched either the ground or the obstacle and the ground.

vii. **Knocking down a fence flag**

There is no penalty for knocking down a boundary or obstacle flag.

If in the process the horse's head passes the wrong side of the flag, i.e. to the left of the white or the right of the red, the competitor must retake the fence and will be debited the penalties for the

Examples of Refusals, Run-outs, Circles (diagrams 1 - 10) and Blacklined Fences (11 & 12)

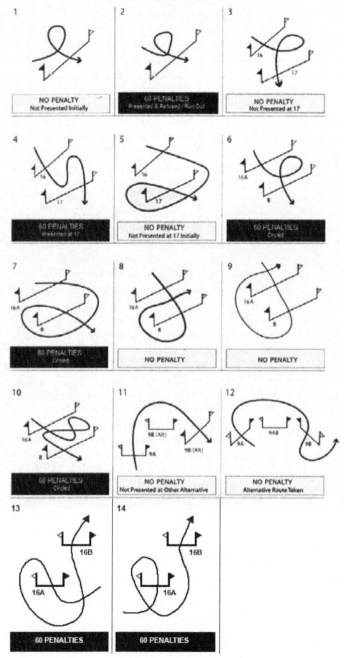

1 — NO PENALTY / Not Presented Initially

2 — 60 PENALTIES / Presented & Refused / Run Out

3 — NO PENALTY / Not Presented at 17

4 — 60 PENALTIES / Presented at 17

5 — NO PENALTY / Not Presented at 17 Initially

6 — 60 PENALTIES / Circled

7 — 60 PENALTIES / Circled

8 — NO PENALTY

9 — NO PENALTY

10 — 60 PENALTIES / Circled

11 — NO PENALTY / Not Presented at Other Alternative

12 — NO PENALTY / Alternative Route Taken

13 — 60 PENALTIES

14 — 60 PENALTIES

run out(s). Competitors may ask if they have to retake the fence, and the Fence Judge is obliged to tell them. This is not considered 'Forbidden Assistance'. Flags do not have to be replaced by Fence Judges but riders may request that flags are replaced. The time will not be stopped for competitors during replacement of a flag.

viii. There is no penalty for jumping a fence which is NOT included on the course but the penalty for jumping a fence marked with crossed flags is disqualification.

ix. As explained in rule h. i) Jumping an obstacle in the wrong direction will result in mandatory retirement.

j.　　Overtaking

Any competitor who is about to be overtaken by a following competitor must quickly clear the way. Any competitor overtaking another competitor must do so only at a safe and suitable place. When the leading competitor is before an obstacle and about to be overtaken, they must follow the directions of the Fence Judge. When the leading competitor is committed to jumping an obstacle, the following competitor may only jump that obstacle in such a way that will cause no inconvenience or danger for either.

The penalty for wilful obstruction of an overtaking competitor, or failure to follow the instructions of the Fence Judge, or causing danger to another competitor, is disqualification at the discretion of the Official Steward.

k.　　Competitor in difficulty at an obstacle

A competitor in difficulty or likely to cause an obstruction must give way to the following horse by quickly clearing away from the front of the obstacle. If, in attempting to negotiate an obstacle, a horse should be trapped in such a way that it is liable to injure itself or be unable to proceed without assistance, the competitor will be instructed to dismount and must retire.

A competitor negotiating the gate or slip rail may continue until their 60 seconds have elapsed, in which case a succeeding competitor will be given an allowance for the time during which they are held up.

l.　　Stopping Competitors

If any part of an obstacle is obstructed by a competitor in difficulty, or if any obstacle has been dismantled to release a fallen horse, or if an obstacle has been broken and is not yet rebuilt, or in any other similar circumstances, and competitor approaching the jump, and any subsequent competitors, must be prepared to stop on the instructions of the Fence Judge, who will wave a flag at waist height in the path of the oncoming competitor. The time during which the competitor is stopped will be noted by the Fence Judge and will be deducted from the time taken to give their correct time for completing the course. Failure to stop is penalised by disqualification at the discretion of the Official Steward.

m.   **Forbidden Assistance**

Outside assistance is forbidden under penalty of disqualification. Any intervention by a third party, whether solicited or not, with the object of facilitating the task of the competitor or of helping their horse is considered forbidden assistance. If in the opinion of the Official Steward, the assistance was unsolicited and the competitor gained no advantage then no penalty will apply.

In particular the following are forbidden:

- **i.**   to intentionally join another competitor and to continue the course in company with them.
- **ii.**   to post friends at certain points to call directions or make signals in passing.
- **iii.** for anyone at an obstacle actively to encourage the horse or rider by any means whatsoever.
- **iv.**   to be followed, preceded or accompanied on any part of the course by any other person
- **v.**   to receive any information, by any means whatsoever, about the course before it is officially open to the competitors.
- **vi.**   for a Fence Judge or official to call back or assist a competitor by directions to rectify an error of course.

EXCEPTIONS: After a fall, or if a competitor dismounts, they may be assisted to catch their horse, to adjust their saddlery, to remount or be handed any part of their equipment while they are dismounted, or after they have remounted. **Fence judges are under no obligation to help a member remount.** Whips, headgear or spectacles may be handed to a competitor without them dismounting. Fence Judges are allowed to call 1st Refusal, 2nd Refusal etc.

When a competitor has been awarded a 60 second failure at a gate or slip–rail, the Judge shall inform them and tell them to proceed to the next obstacle, and if necessary explain the by–pass route to them.

n.   **Retirement**

Competitors retiring from any part of the Cross Country course for any reason whatsoever must leave the course at a walk and take every precaution to avoid disturbing other competitors. They may not jump any obstacles after retiring.

o.   Obstacles

i.   Obstacles must be solid, fixed and imposing. Where natural obstacles are used, they must be reinforced if necessary, so that they present, as far as possible, the same problem throughout the competition.

ii.   Obstacles will be numbered and flagged and must be jumped in numerical and/or alphabetical order

iii. Obstacles should be designed within the limits of the different Levels to prepare competitors for the Championships, using 'L' fences or black line alternatives to avoid retirement for the less experienced. All obstacles must be sited so that a vehicle can get to them to evacuate casualties.

p.   Dimensions

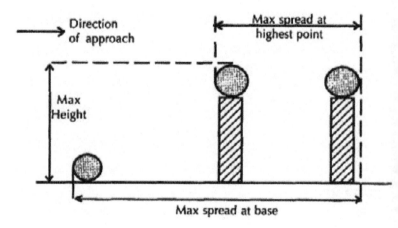

i.   Obstacles are measured from the point from which the average horse would normally take off.

ii.   When measuring the height of an obstacle it does not mean that obstacles must always be of uniform height or spread throughout their length, or that these dimensions may never be exceeded anywhere between the Red and White flags marking the extent of an obstacle. It is sufficient if that part of the obstacle, where the average horse and rider could reasonably and conveniently be expected to jump does not exceed the maximum permitted dimensions.

iii. Obstacles with spread only (stream, ditch, etc.) must not exceed the dimensions given in the table. A low rail or hedge, provided that it merely facilitates the jumping of the obstacle, is not considered to give height to this type of obstacle.

iv. Obstacles with both height and spread (oxer, open ditch, etc.) are measured both at the base from the outside of the relevant rails or other material making up the obstacle, and at the top from the outside of the relevant rails or other material making up the highest points (see diagram). The spread of an obstacle at its top is measured from the outside of the relevant rails or other material making up the obstacle at the highest points.

v. In the case of an obstacle where the height cannot be clearly defined (natural hedge, brush fence) the measurement is taken to the fixed and solid part of the obstacle through which a horse cannot pass with impunity and which must be visible from the front. The overall height of a natural hedge or brush fence may not exceed the maximum height by more than 20cm.

vi. Poles used for timber obstacles shall not be less than 10cm in diameter at their narrower end.

q. Alternative 'L' Obstacles

The primary purpose of alternative 'L' obstacles is to enable the course builder to build a course at the right standard but which the less experienced competitor can complete.

i. At Area competitions and Branch events 'L' obstacles will be provided as alternatives to some of the more difficult 'Main' obstacles and will be separate from them. 'L' fences and black line flags will be used at both Area competitions and the Championships.

ii. An 'L' obstacle may be an alternative to either a single or multiple 'main' obstacle, but need not have the same number of elements.

iii. In a multiple obstacle, after jumping one or more elements of the 'main' obstacle, a competitor may change to the 'L' element of the alternative obstacle that is next in sequence and vice versa.

iv. It is NOT necessary to go back and jump the 'L' elements of an obstacle when they have already jumped the corresponding 'main' elements, but a competitor is at liberty to do so if they wish.

Marking

v. 'L' obstacles and all 'L' elements in a multiple obstacle will be marked with red and white boundary flags, and with a marker having a red 'L' on a white background beneath the fence number.

vi. Each 'L' obstacle will also be marked with the same number as the corresponding 'main' obstacle. In the case of a multiple obstacle, each 'L' element will have the same letter as the corresponding element of the 'main' obstacle. However, when the 'L' obstacle has fewer elements than the 'main' obstacle, its last element will be marked with all the remaining corresponding letters.

Penalties

vii. Jumping **or attempting** an alternative 'L' obstacle or any part of it will incur a penalty of 70 points only (regardless of the number of elements) in addition to any penalties for refusals, falls, etc.

viii. Penalties incurred at the 'main' obstacle and those at its alternative 'L' obstacle are cumulative.

r.   **Adjacent Obstacles**

If two or more obstacles, although sited close together, are designed as separate problems, each will be numbered and judged independently. A competitor may circle between them without penalty, provided that this is not as a result of attempting to negotiate the next obstacle. They must not, under penalty of disqualification, retake any obstacle they have already jumped.

s.   **Combination Fences**

If an obstacle is formed of several elements, each part shall be flagged and marked with a different letter (A, B, C, etc.) but only the first element shall be numbered and all elements will be judged as one obstacle. They must be jumped in the correct sequence.

A competitor who circles between two lettered elements incurs penalties. They may refuse, run out or circle only twice in all without having to retire. The third refusal within the obstacle as a whole incurs retirement. If a competitor refuses or falls off at any element they are permitted to retake any elements already jumped, although they will be penalised for any new fault even if they have previously jumped an element successfully. A competitor may pass the wrong way through the flags of any element in order to retake an element.

t.   **Banks** onto the top of which a horse is intended to jump may not exceed the maximum height for the relevant Level given in the table below. If the slope is sufficient to allow a horse to land on the face and scramble up, there is no limit to the height or spread.

u.   **Bounces** – Double bounces are NOT allowed, except at steps. Single bounces, if included, must have an easier alternative that may or may not be an 'L'. If there is an alternative route, as opposed to an 'L' option, both sets of flags must be marked with a black line.

Judging of bounce obstacles:

At any obstacle where the distance between elements is 5 metres or less (i.e. a bounce) when a horse has negotiated the first element without penalty, it will be deemed to have been presented at the second element and similarly if the bounce is for example the second and third elements of a combination. Thus if a rider changes their mind while negotiating the first element of a bounce, and for example then goes a longer route, they will still be penalised 60 penalties for a run–out.

v.   **Bullfinches –** are NOT allowed, as they cannot be maintained in the same condition all day.

w.   **Drop** should be measured from the highest point of the obstacle to where the average horse would normally land.

x.   **Open Ditches** (i.e. ditches on the take off side of the fence) must be clearly defined. If they have no guard rail they should be revetted on the take off side.

y.   **Water Obstacles**

   i.   Water obstacles which require a horse to jump into water either over a fence or down a vertical drop may be included, provided there is an alternative 'L' obstacle and the underwater surface is sound. Where no alternative is provided, the entrance into the water must be a gradual slope with no fence or drop.

   ii.   In both cases the water must be at least 6m wide to ensure that a bold horse does not attempt to jump it and not deeper than 20cm, measured at the point at which the average horse would land. Likewise the water must not exceed this depth where the average horse would take off. Elsewhere the water should not greatly exceed this depth.

z.   **Hazards**

Certain natural features such as ditches and "drops", which, although not regarded as obstacles and therefore not numbered, might cause some horses to refuse may be classified as hazards. Their dimensions must not exceed the maximum allowed for other obstacles. Refusals, run–outs, circles and falls are not penalised at hazards. The only penalty is retirement if the horse resists its rider for 60 consecutive seconds. Riders may not dismount and lead through or over a hazard on penalty of retirement.

aa. Practice Fence

There will be a simple practice fence for warming up near the start, marked with red and white flags, which must be jumped with the red flag on the right. Only fences that are marked with red and white flags may be jumped in the warm–up area. Practice fences must not exceed the maximum dimensions allowed for the class.

bb. Gate and Slip Rail

If the gate and slip rail are not in an existing fence, a length of fencing must be constructed, extending about 3 metres (or more) on either side. The gate should open in one direction only and where at all possible, in the direction of travel of horse and rider. **No more than one slip rail should be available for competitors to use.**

The slip rail will be between 91cm and 1.22m high. There will also be a lower rail, to be negotiated (dismounted) without taking it down, about 30cm high. A mounting block should be provided for optional use without penalty by all competitors. It should be fit for purpose, sturdy and structurally stable, and checked regularly by fence judges to ensure it remains in a consistently safe and stable condition. Should a hay or straw bale be utilised, spare bales should be available on site to replace a bale that is losing its structure.

cc. In bad weather, or where space or budget restricts, an Arena Jumping course may replace the Cross Country riding phase – see Appendix C. Qualification for the Championships must be at the Chairman's discretion if a Cross Country phase is not completed.

dd. Frangible pins and MIMS Clips

    i.   If a BE course is being used and you wish to use a fence with a frangible pin you must make sure that there is an accredited course builder present to deal with it should a pin be broken. It should be remembered that the Frangible Pin system has been designed to activate under certain circumstances. The version currently in use has been designed in line with the weight of an average horse (470kg).

  ii.   **MIMS Clips**

        If a BE course is being used includes a fence with MIMS clips, ensure that there is an accredited course builder there to deal with it should a clip need to be replaced.

25. OBSTACLES – MAXIMUM AND MINIMUM HEIGHTS FOR COMPETITION LEVELS

	Minimus (PC80)	Junior (PC90)	Intermediate (PC100)	Open (PC110)
Length of Course	The length of the course shall be between 1600–3000m at Area competitions and 2000–3500m at the championships.			
Speed	Not to be timed	450mpm	475mpm	475mpm
Maximum Height	0.80m	0.90m	1.00m	1.00m (1.05m at the Championships)
Number of Obstacles (jumping efforts) Maximum	25 jumping efforts excluding gate and slip rail increasing to 30 at International and Championship competitions			
Minimum	18 jumping efforts excluding gate and slip rail 3 'L' Obstacles or black flag alternatives* All courses must include a gate and slip rail			
Maximum height and Spread Max. spread highest point	0.90m	1.00m	1.10m	1.10m
Max spread base	1.25m	1.50m	1.80m	1.80m
With Spread Only Maximum spread without height	1.00m	1.20m	1.80m	1.80m

Drop Fences Maximum Drop	1.20m	1.30m	1.40m	1.40m
Jump into and out of water Max depth of water	0.20m	0.20m	0.20m	0.20m

26.   SCORING

a. 1400 Marks are awarded for a clear round within the time allowed. Riders who fail to complete the course shall retain credit for that part of the course which they have completed before retiring.

b. The score for a rider who does not complete the course shall be calculated by totalling:

i. 500 penalties for retirement.

ii. Any jumping penalties incurred BEFORE the point of retirement.

iii. 50 penalties for each fence BEYOND the point of retirement, i.e. fences which the rider has not attempted.

(This must include 50 penalties for any obstacle BEYOND the point of retirement which may have been taken out of the course and subtracting this total from 1400 (should this total exceed 1400 the rider shall score zero).

c.   Retirement conditions

i. Where retirement is as a result of a rider failing to negotiate an obstacle, the ONLY penalty incurred at that obstacle shall be the 500 points for retirement, regardless of how many jumping penalties may have been incurred at that obstacle in leading up to the compulsory retirement.

ii. If a rider retires BETWEEN fences, either voluntarily or compulsorily the fence TOWARDS which they were, or should have been, riding shall be taken as the fence at which the 500 points for retirement were incurred. Should the retirement occur between the final fence and the finish, or should the rider simply omit to pass through the finishing flags and fail to correct the error, the 500 point penalty shall be awarded.

iii. A rider who retires, for any reason, before attempting the THIRD obstacle on the course shall score zero for the riding phase.

iv. At Area Competitions: in cases of genuine lameness (certified by either a Veterinary Surgeon or the Official Steward), a competitor shall score zero for the riding phase.

27.   SPECIAL CONDITIONS

a.   A competitor continuing the course after being required to retire may be disqualified unless there are considered to be extenuating circumstances such as doubt on their part as to the award of a refusal. The Chief Scorer will report such cases, as will any Official to whom they are evident.

b.   If a competitor is unable to mount after the slip rail they may receive assistance to do so but will incur **70** penalties. **Fence judges are under no obligation to help a member remount.**

c.   The maximum penalty (other than for falls) which can be incurred at the gate or slip rail is 260.

d.   In exceptional circumstances, and only with the approval of the Official Steward, competitors held on the course may be allowed to warm up over a previous fence at Area level and above.

RUNNING – RULES

28.   GENERAL

a.   The running phase may be held using either a mass start, where several competitors set off at the same time, as in a race; or as a time trial, where each competitor starts alone, usually 1 minute apart. The method being employed must be stated on the schedule and/or entry form in advance of the competition. The event programme should inform competitors of their individual or heat start time so that they may warm up accordingly.

b.   A competitor may be given instructions, encouragement or information whilst running but nobody may run with or near them or act as a pacemaker. A penalty of 30 seconds will be incurred for each breach of this rule.

c.   Dress – Competitors should as a minimum wear shorts and a running vest, and may not run stripped to the waist.

d.   Personal electronic devices capable of playing music may not be used.

29.   THE COURSE

a.   A simple plan of the course should be made available at the start. If more than one lap is to be run to make up the required distance, then this should be clearly indicated.

b.   **Flagging / Marking** – The course should be clearly marked using red and white flags, which must be respected under penalty of retirement. Should the Official Steward, in conjunction with the Run Phase Steward, conclude that a flag was inadvertently missed, they may award a 15 second penalty for each flag missed, in lieu of a requirement to retire.

c.   Distance markers should be placed every 500 metres.

d.   Where a single number is used runners must wear this on their front. Otherwise a number should be worn front and back.

30.   PROCEDURE AND TIMING – TIME TRIALS

a.   Competitors must be despatched at 1 minute intervals and timed from the moment they leave the start until they cross the finishing line. The method is to record the time at which each runner starts and finishes and subtract one from the other to determine the time taken.

31.   PROCEDURE AND TIMING – MASS STARTS

a.   Separate heats should be used for different classes. However, when there are a small number of competitors in a class then it may be merged with another class competing over the same distance. Individual heats should not exceed 12 runners. If there is a false start the runners will be recalled and the heat restarted.

32.   SCORING

The standard times for which a score of 1000 points is awarded are shown below. At all levels of competition, 3 points per second are added/subtracted for each second under/over the standard. The Open Boys deduction reduces to 1 point per second after 13 minutes 16 seconds.

- ▸ **Open Boys (3,000 metres)**
  10 minutes 30 seconds
- ▸ **Open and Intermediate Girls (1,500 metres)**
  5 minutes 20 seconds
- ▸ **Intermediate Boys (2,000 metres)**
  7 minutes 0 seconds

- **Junior Boys (1,500 metres)**
  5 minutes 10 seconds
- **Junior Girls (1,500 metres)**
  5 minutes 40 seconds
- **Minimus Boys and Girls (1,000 metres)**
  4 minutes 0 seconds
- **Tadpole Boys and Girls (1,000 metres)**
  4 minutes 0 seconds
- **Beanies Boys and Girls (500 metres)**
  2 minutes 0 seconds

SHOOTING – RULES

Note: These rules are in line with current legislation with regard to firearm laws at the time of print. Any changes will be noted on The Pony Club website.

33.   GENERAL

a.   A competitor is to wear normal athletic or everyday clothing. Long trousers are required.

b.   The use of any special devices, means or garments which support the competitor's leg, body or arms is prohibited.

c.   Substantial shoes (that do not reach the anklebone but which cover the whole foot – e.g. trainers) must be worn.

d.   Wristbands or similar items that might provide support are prohibited on the hand(s) and arm(s) holding the pistol.

e.   Protective or prescription glasses are recommended at all levels and are mandatory for shooting at 7 metres. Any type of sound producing or communication system is prohibited. Sound reducing devices (ear defenders or ear plugs), visors, caps, eye patches, corrective lenses or filter may be worn.

f.   Pistols are to be held in one hand only for Open, Intermediate and Junior competitions. The other hand or arm may not be used to hold or support the pistol, the pistol hand or any part of the pistol arm.

g.   For Minimus competitions the pistol may be held in two hands. No part of either hand should be forward of the trigger guard.

h.   Firing will be from an erect standing unsupported position.

i.   No person (Coach, Parent or Competitor) is permitted to use optical instruments, such as field glasses, binoculars, cameras and spotting scopes, during a competitor's shoot except during the sighting/practice shots.

j.   At the firing point, range supervision is provided by the **Range Conducting Officer** acting as the Chief Range Officer.

k.   A competitor does not need to be supported by an adult. Any competitor may load their pistol themselves (i.e. without a loader) if they wish and are deemed safe and competent by the **Range Conducting Officer**. If not, the **Range Conducting Officer** may request a loader to support an individual shooter.

l.   All entries for shooting must be signed off prior to shooting as being competent to shoot at competitions by the Team Manager.

34.   SAFETY

a.   An outline of the Law Relating to Air Pistols will be found at Appendix B. Contravention of the Law or these Rules by a competitor may lead to individual or team disqualification at the sole discretion of the Official Steward, whose decision is final and may not be appealed.

b.   No person under 18 years of age may be in possession of or carry an air pistol or pellets in a public place, unless that person is under the supervision of someone over 21 years.

c.   Charging air and gas pistol cylinders should be handled by responsible persons only and charging cylinders should be kept safely in a secure area before and during a competition. Junior and Minimus competitors must be supervised when charging air pistol cylinders by an official or delegated responsible person.

d.   No person under the age of 8 (on the day of competition) may shoot at a Pony Club event, including postal pistol competitions.

e.   It is mandatory for at least one qualified Range Officer (e.g. NSRA Range Conducting Officer, NSRA Youth Proficiency Scheme Pistol Tutor) to be in overall charge of the Range for all Pony Club shooting occasions (competitions or practice). The Range Officer's primary role is to ensure safety procedures are followed by everyone in the vicinity of the Range, (e.g. athletes, coaches, spectators & officials) and must be over 21 years old with prior experience/knowledge of Pony Club shooting.

f.   Approved Shooting Qualifications for Pony Club Range Officers: The National Smallbore Rifle Association (NSRA) runs courses for the following approved qualifications which are renewable every 5 years:

- **Range Conducting Officer (RCO)**

- **Youth Proficiency Scheme (YSP) Pistol Tutor**

Coaches holding NSRA Club Instructor, Club Coach, County Coach or Regional Coach qualifications can be a Range Officer on a Pony Club Range as they include an RCO qualification, although this may need confirmation if not co-terminus with the Coaching renewal.

g.   At a shooting range and environs pistols must be kept in their cases until the **Range Conducting Officer** gives the order to "unbox" them at the start of a detail, and they must be "boxed" again before the competitors leave the Firing Point.

h.   Pistols are loaded only at the Firing Point and only after the command "LOAD" is given.

i.   If any of the Range Staff considers that there is a potential or actual breach of safety which urgently requires all firers to stop firing that person will immediately give the order "Stop, Stop, Stop". All firers must immediately stop firing, take their finger off the trigger, lower the pistol to the starting position and await further instructions. Loaders, are to keep fingers away from the trigger, immediately stop what they are doing and await further instructions from the **Range Conducting Officer**.

The person ordering the stop, if not the **Range Conducting Officer**, must immediately explain their action to the FPS so that they may take effective control of the situation.

j.   Safety flags (safety line can be strimmer cord), must be inserted in all pistols at all times except when the safety flag removal is authorised by the **Range Conducting Officer**. To demonstrate that air guns are unloaded, safety flags (safety lines) must be long enough to extend through the full length of the barrel.

Safety flags must be inserted:

- at any time the pistol is unboxed. (Preferably safety flag will be in place when pistol is removed from the box)

- when anyone is forward of the firing point. (e.g. changing targets)

- upon completion of firing detail. (The pistol is considered safe and ready to be boxed with action open, safety flag in place (to confirm no pellet in the barrel) and confirmed as safe to box by the **Range Conducting Officer**)

- anytime instructed to by the **Range Conducting Officer**.

35. TARGETS

a. Only the official target obtainable from The Pony Club Shop is to be used for all Official Competitions.

b. Targets should be placed in a row with the centre of the target 134cm above the ground and a minimum of 0.56m apart. They should not be sited directly against a hard vertical background so as to avoid pellet ricochet.

c. The distance between the target and the front foot of the competitor is to be 10m (+/– 5cm (2 inches) for Open and Intermediate and 7m(+/– 5cm (2 inches) for Junior and Minimus competitions.

d. Only one target per competitor should be exposed at the same time.

36. EQUIPMENT

a. The equipment for Shooting consists of the pistol only. If a competitor wishes to use any accessory they must have it examined and approved by the Chief Steward (or a shooting official nominated by them) of the phase before the detail begins. The use of accessories and equipment that are contrary to the spirit of these rules is forbidden.

b. Pistols can be of any make of 'low powered' 4.5mm (.177 inch) calibre air pistol powered by spring/pneumatic, compressed air or CO_2 provided a firearms certificate is not required. Different rules apply in N.I. and Scotland. No magazine for loading more than one pellet is allowed. A low powered air pistol is defined as one generating less that 8.1Joules (6ft lbs) in the UK.

c. The competitor is responsible for presenting all pistols and equipment and/or accessories for official inspection and approval prior to the event. The competitor must use the same pistol in all shots of the event unless it ceases to function. If the competitor begins or completes the competition with an unapproved pistol he/she must be disqualified.

d. After the equipment has been approved, the pistol is not to be modified or adjusted (other than adjustment of sight alignment) at any time prior to or during the event nor must it be exchanged if in safe working order. Any alterations or adjusting of the officially approved pistol so that it violates the rules, or exchange without approval, will incur disqualification. If there are any doubts regarding any alteration, the pistol must be returned to the Chief Steward (or a shooting official nominated by them) for re–inspection and approval prior to the start of the competitor's shooting detail.

e.   Pellets must be 4.5mm (.177 inch) calibre of soft lead and be of 'wad cutter' type (flat nosed). Diablo, steel and composite type pellets are prohibited. Pellets should be submitted for inspection with other equipment prior to the start of shooting.

f.   Adjustable grips are permitted.

g.   Only black coloured, open sights are allowed. Optical, mirror, telescopic, laser beam, electronically projected dot, optically enhanced sights etc. are prohibited. A protective covering over the front or rear sight to facilitate cocking of the pistol does not infringe this rule.

h.   Corrective lenses and/or filters must not be attached to the pistol but may be worn by the competitor.

i.   No part of the grip or accessories is to encircle the hand or extend in any way which would give any support beyond the hand.

j.   Pistols must be checked as to calibre and dimension. All approved equipment must be marked with a seal or sticker that will be valid only for the respective competition.

k.   The pistol together with all accessories must be capable of fitting into a control box measuring 420mm long by 200mm wide and 50mm deep at any time.

l.   All mobile phones and any other type of communication system must be switched off whilst in the range and range environs. This applies to athletes, officials, spectators and all other persons with no exception.

37.   METHOD – COURSE OF FIRE

a.   Each competitor will have two targets each of 5 shots fired consecutively and with a time limit of a 4 second target exposure per shot.

b.   Prior to the two competitive competition targets, competitors should be allowed 5 sighting/practice shots at a static practice target.

c.   Coaching is allowed during the firing of sighting/practice shots. No communication of any nature between the competitor and any other person, with the exception of the shooting officials, is allowed once the firing of competition shots has commenced.

d.   Loaders (who must be aged 18 or over) may be used.

e.   Loaders / target changers are required to stand back at least two metres behind the competitor after loading / changing the targets.

f.   Having loaded, until the targets are exposed or the order to "Fire" is given competitors must hold their pistols at arm's length at an angle of at least 45 degrees below the horizontal or with barrel muzzles resting on the tables provided, at the option of each competitor.

g.   If a pistol powered by an air/CO_2 cylinder or cartridge is used, it is the responsibility of the competitor to ensure that they have sufficient air to complete the series of shots including sighting shots.

38.   RANGE COMMANDS

a.   The following range commands are to be used:

- "Load"
- "Are you Ready"

(If not, then competitors must immediately say they are not)

- Mechanically exposed target: "Watch and Shoot"
- Continuously exposed targets: "Stand by"

After a pause of approximately 3-4 seconds

- Targets are exposed for 4 seconds: "Fire"

After 4 seconds (during which time competitors fire one shot)

- Competitors fire one shot: "Stop"
- "Reload"
- "Are you Ready", etc.

(At end of Series)

- "Cease Fire"
- "Unload"
- "Bench Pistols" (ensure 'safe' condition)
- "Change / Collect Targets"

b.   If, due to an incorrect command and/or action by the **Range Conducting Officer**, the competitor is not ready to fire when the command "Watch and Shoot" or "Fire" is given, they must hold their pistol pointing down the range, raise their free hand, and report the situation to the **Range Conducting Officer**. They must not disturb other competitors. If the claim is justified the competitor must be allowed to fire the shot with the next regular shot. At the end of the series the competitor will complete their series as necessary. If the claim is unjustified, the shot is lost and scores zero.

If the competitor has fired a shot after the incorrect command and/or incorrect action, a protest will not be accepted and the shot is scored.

39.   SCORING

a.   All scoring targets will be collected by an official and must not be shown either to the competitor or team officials before they have been scored. All scoring should be conducted by two Scorers and a Scrutineer. The Phase Steward should not be the Scrutineer. Scoring should take place in a location remote from other competition officials and access to scorers should be restricted to other officials. The Scorers and Scrutineer shall report directly to the Shoot Phase Steward.

b.   The scores are:

▸   10 points for a Bull
▸   8 points for an Inner
▸   6 points for a Magpie
▸   4 points for an Outer
▸   2 points for outside the Outer scoring ring
▸   0 points for the quarter inch outer border

c.   If any part of a higher value scoring ring or area is touched by the pellet, the shot must be scored the higher value of the two scoring rings. This is determined by whether either the pellet hole (where it is clearly defined) or a plug or overlay gauge (if there is any doubt that the pellet hole does not clearly define the passage of the pellet through the target) inserted in or over the hole touches any part of the outside edge of the scoring ring.

d.   On mechanically exposed targets, shots fired whilst the target is turning and causing an elongated hole over 6 mm long are scored as zero.

e.   If, when targets are continuously exposed, the competitor exceeds the time limit of 4 seconds per shot, the highest scoring shot (or shots, if exceeded more than once) shall be subtracted from the total scored on the target or targets concerned. The **Range Conducting Officer** shall verbally inform the competitor on each occurrence after the command "Stop". The decision of the **Range Conducting Officer** is final and may not be appealed and no shot may be repeated.

f.   Each competitor's total target score is to be multiplied by 10 to calculate the total number of points scored in the shooting phase.

g.   If more than 5 shots appear on a target and it is adjudicated that the extra shot could not have been fired by that competitor, then the competitor will be credited with the highest 5 (five) scoring shots on the target.

If the competitor has (or believes they have) loaded more than one pellet on the command to "load" then they should retain a grip on and keep the pistol pointing down range and inform the **Range Conducting Officer**. They will be given an opportunity to either discharge the pistol in a safe direction (not pointing) at the targets or remove the pellets from the breech and loading chamber before the next regular shot. They shall complete the series under direction of the **Range Conducting Officer**.

If a competitor fires more than one pellet (for whatever reason) at a single target exposure or on the command to "fire" using static targets then they will score the 5 lowest scoring shots in the series.

h.   If the Scorers do not agree on either the value of a shot or number of shots on a target, a decision from the Scrutineer must be requested immediately.

A plug gauge may be inserted only once in any single pellet hole and only by the Scrutineer in the presence of the Scorers. The use of a plug gauge must be marked on the target by the Scorers and Scrutineer, together with their initials, and showing the result. The use of a skid shot gauge should also be recorded on the target.

The Scrutineer may, in the presence of the Scorers, use a 'double shot' hole gauge, approved in advance by the Phase Steward, to help adjudicate possible multiple shots in a single hole. This gauge may only be used as a last resort after all other permitted scoring gauges and methods have been used. The scoring decision of the Scrutineer is final and may not be appealed.

i.   Once the targets have been scored, they are to be made available for checking by one authorised representative of the competitor. They must be checked in the presence of one of the event organisers in the collection area and signed off. If targets are removed from the inspection area for whatever reason prior to being signed off, the score as given must stand. No gauges or other scoring equipment shall be used by anyone other than the Scrutineer.

j.　　　The authorised representative may appeal entries in the results list, score card totals and the value of any single shot hole in which a plug gauge has not been previously inserted. The Scrutineer and Scorers will consider all appeals working alone and their decision is final.

40.　　PISTOL MALFUNCTIONS

a.　　　If a shot has not fired due to pistol malfunction, and if the competitor wishes to claim a malfunction, they must hold their pistol pointing down the range, retain their grip, and immediately inform the **Range Conducting Officer** by raising their free hand. They must not disturb other competitors. A competitor may try to correct a malfunction or continue the shot, but if they do and the shot is lost, they may not claim a malfunction and the shot shall be scored as zero.

b.　　　When determining the cause of a malfunction, if the external appearance of the pistol does not show an obvious reason for the malfunction, the **Range Conducting Officer** must take the pistol carefully and safely from the competitor. The **Range Conducting Officer** must not interfere with nor touch the loading mechanism but point the pistol in a safe direction and pull the trigger once only to determine whether the trigger mechanism had been released. If the pistol does not discharge the **Range Conducting Officer** must complete the examination of the pistol to determine the cause of the malfunction and decide whether or not the malfunction is allowable.

c.　　　A malfunction of a pistol is considered as allowable when a part of the pistol has failed and, in particular:

  i.　　A pellet sticks in the barrel (unless due to insufficient air or gas under the control of the competitor)
  ii.　　The trigger mechanism has failed to operate
  iii.　There is a pellet in the chamber and the trigger mechanism has been released and operated
  iv.　The pistol has "jammed"
  v.　　Any part of the pistol is damaged sufficiently to prevent the pistol from functioning (unless under the control of the competitor).

If after inspection of the pistol, the **Range Conducting Officer** decides that there was an allowable malfunction the competitor has the right to fire an additional shot concurrent with the next regular shot or at the end of the regular series as appropriate under command of the **Range Conducting**

Officer. A malfunction is allowed twice in the course of the competition. Any subsequent pistol malfunction shall be scored as zero.

If the pistol is inoperable then the competitor may repeat the lost shots as part of a subsequent detail with an approved exchange pistol. The competitor may fire additional practice/sighting shots on their allocated detail. They shall complete the required number of shots at the beginning of the series only.

d.   A malfunction is considered as non–allowable when it is the competitor's fault and in particular:

i.   The competitor or another person has touched the pistol before it is inspected by the **Range Conducting Officer**.

ii.   The safety catch had not been released or had gone on "safe" during shooting.

iii.   The competitor had not loaded the pistol.

iv.   The pistol had been loaded with the wrong pellets.

v.   The pistol had run out of air or CO_2 (except due to malfunction of the propellant mechanism).

vi.   The malfunction was due to any other cause that could reasonably have been controlled by the competitor.

If after inspection of the pistol, the **Range Conducting Officer** decides that a malfunction was non–allowable, the competitor loses that shot and scores zero.

41.   SHOOTING IRREGULARITIES AND INFRINGEMENTS

a.   A competitor must not raise their pistol before either the target faces or the command "fire" on static targets.

b.   If a pistol powered by an air/CO_2 cylinder or cartridge is used, the competitor may not change the cylinder or cartridge during the competition.

c.   If a pellet is discharged accidentally after the command "Watch and Shoot" or "Standby" that shot is lost.

d.   If a pellet is discharged accidentally after the command "Load" and before either the command "Watch and Shoot" or "Standby' the shooter shall wait and fire any additional shot at the end of the regular series under command of the **Range Conducting Officer**. Any subsequent occurrence in the series of competition shots shall be scored as zero.

e.   A competitor who fires a shot before the command "Load" must be disqualified.

f. The **Range Conducting Officer** shall enter all malfunctions and irregularities on the range register and send a note with the relevant target to the Scrutineers. Should doubt persist, the **Range Conducting Officer** should meet with the Scrutineers after the end of shooting and before the score for the relevant target is finalised.

SWIMMING – RULES

42. GENERAL

Competitors will score points according to the distance swum. They may use whatever style they wish and may change it during the swim.

43. METHOD

a. Competitors should swim in heats, the number in each heat depending on the width of the pool.

b. A Competitor may start the swim already in the water provided they are in contact with the end of the pool by at least one hand or foot.

c. Diving

Competitors who wish to dive, either from blocks or from the side of the pool, will need to have the relevant Diving Certificate. Note there is no restriction on competitors starting in the water.

Diving Certificate	
Swimming Teachers Association Competitive Starts and Turns Level 1	Able to dive into pool from poolside/blocks - depth 1.5 metres.
Swim England Preliminary Competitive Start Award	
Swimming Teachers Association Competitive Starts and Turns Level 2	Able to dive into the pool from poolside/blocks - Depth 1.35 metres
Competitive Start Award	

To dive from blocks/poolside there is a requirement to have a signed and dated certificate from a Swimming Coach with a qualification from below:

Qualification	Diving Certificate
▸ A Swim England Coach or Senior Coach (or equivalent version as per the swim mark matrix) ▸ A level 2 Swimming Teacher who has also completed the Competitive Starts CPD ▸ A PE Teacher with the Teacher of School Swimming certificate and completed a Competitive Starts CPD	Swim England Competitive Start Awards
▸ Minimum Level 2 Swimming Coach	Swimming Teachers Association Competitive Starts and Turns Award

Tetrathlon managers should order their required number of certificates and make sure they are signed off by an appropriate coach ahead of any competitions.

Competitors should still be able to show a certificate ahead of the swim. It is up to the organiser what format they require the certificate in (digital or physical). The organiser wiil decide how the competitors will be differentiated between their Diving Certificates. Information on how this is differentiated must be included in the schedules.

Branches/Centres should upload the achievement and certificate onto Pelham as a record of the Diving Certificate. Competitors should still be able to show the certificate if asked.

d. The Start

i. The Starter shall take up position at the side of the pool. The competitors, on a signal from the starter, shall take up position a short pace back from the edge of the pool; on the preparatory command from the starter 'Take your marks', the competitors shall immediately take up a starting position on the edge of the pool, and remain motionless until the signal to start; they may not swing their arms or make anticipatory movements of the body, though they may provide any attitude that they wish. If a false start occurs, the starters whistle will be blown for a second time and a stop rope should be deployed. The swimmers must be recalled and the heat restarted.

ii.   If the first attempt to start the heat is false, the swimmers must be warned that in the event of any further false starts those deemed responsible will be required to start in the water for all subsequent restarts.

e.   The time is taken from the whistle and a whistle will blow to signal the end of the period. The timekeeper should indicate when half time has elapsed and the last 30 seconds of the swim should be counted down in 10 second intervals and the last 10 seconds in single seconds.

f.   A swimmer must touch the end of the pool with some part of their body each time they turn, and 50 pts. will be deducted each time they fail to do so **as monitored by the turn/lane judge**.

Note: Swim England rules as to how the end is to be touched, depending on the style of swim, do not apply.

As the starter counts down to the end of the swim, if a competitor is close to completing a length and the competitor begins a tumble turn, it is the lane judge's discretion to decide if that length has been completed before the final whistle. If a competitor completes a tumble turn they are considered to have completed that length. The lane judge should also determine if any extra meters were gained before the final whistle, after the turn was completed.

g.   The distance swum is measured at the point reached by the foremost part of the swimmer's person when the whistle is blown.

44.   COACHES/TEAM TRAINERS

Coaches/Team Trainers are allowed at the end of the pool away from the start to give competitors encouragement and/or information, or coaching during the warm up period. They may not place hands or objects in the water to encourage or aid swimmers, but may do so only by voice. They alone may check **the scoreboard/results page to ensure the lengths swam by the swimmer are correct**.

45.   SCORING

The standard distances for which a score of 1000 points is awarded are show below. At all levels of competition, 3 points per metre are added/subtracted for each metre over/under the standard.

- ‣ **Open Boys (4 minutes)**
  285 metres
- ‣ **Open Girls and Intermediate Boys and Girls (3 minutes)**
  225 metres
- ‣ **Junior Boys and Girls (3 minutes)**
  185 metres
- ‣ **Minimus Boys and Girls (2 minutes)**
  125 metres
- ‣ **Tadpole Boys and Girls (2 minutes)**
  125 metres
- ‣ **Beanies Boys and Girls (2 minutes)**
  125 metres

46.   WALKING

a.   If a competitor is seen to be walking on the bottom of the pool, the Judge shall deduct from the distance covered by that competitor an amount equal to the distance they estimate the competitor walked instead of swam.

b.   There is nothing to prevent a competitor who, for any reason, leaves the pool, re–entering and continuing their swim provided they are within the time and starts again from the point at which they left off.

47.   FORBIDDEN SUBSTANCES

The use of grease, oil or any similar substance on the body is forbidden.

48.   EQUIPMENT

The use of swimming or buoyancy aids is forbidden at any level of competition, although provided the Organiser and Swimming Pool owner agree, Branch competitions may waive this condition for competitors aged 8 years of age or less.

a.   The competitor must only wear one swimsuit, in one or two pieces. Full length swimsuits are accepted.

b.   All swimsuits shall be made from textile material.

PART 3 – AREA COMPETITIONS AND CHAMPIONSHIPS

49.   ELIGIBILITY

a.   The District Commissioner or Centre Proprietor is required to certify that the competitor is a member of their Branch at the closing date for entries and that they and their pony/horse are competent in all phases to compete at the level they are entered for at the Area competition. All entries must be verified by the District Commissioner or Centre Proprietor at Area level and above.

Competitors should have practiced and be competent to shoot on a range and be familiar with the rules of shooting for Pony Club Tetrathlon.

b.   Combination of horse and rider in the Intermediate Competition are NOT eligible if they have competed at an Open Area Tetrathlon competition in previous years.

c.   Horses that are graded British Eventing Advanced (Grade 1) and have competed at OI/AI/A level during the current calendar year are not eligible at any level.

d.   All competitors must be Members of The Pony Club both at the closing date for entries to the competition and at the date of the relevant competition to be eligible to compete at Area qualifying competitions and at the Championships.

e.   Riders or horses who have 'schooled' over the Area or Championship Cross Country courses during the previous two weeks are not eligible to compete. Competing over the course is permissible and does not render the competitor ineligible.

50.   AREA QUALIFYING COMPETITIONS

These may be held as single Area events, or composite events in which two or more Areas take part. In the latter case, each Area will be treated as holding a distinct Area Competition.

a.   From the Area Competitions the following go forward to the Open, Intermediate and Junior Championships:

   i.   The winning team at each such event.
   ii.   Where the same Branch/Centre has won the Area Open, Intermediate or Junior Team competition for two consecutive

years and wins again in the year concerned, the runner up Branch, Centre, provided that their score is at least 10,000.

iii. The two highest–placed competitors who are not in a team which qualifies

iv. If only one team from an Area is entered, that team will go forward provided it completes the Area Competition and scores at least 8,000 for Open and Intermediate and 9,000 for Junior.

v. Where an Area Competition does not have any Teams competing on the day, six individual qualifying places are available.

vi. Runner up teams and individuals will only be invited to the Championships by the Tetrathlon Chairman if entry numbers permit

vii. Where an individual competitor has failed to qualify to go forward to the Championships under any of the above rules and has competed in all four phases AND has a score for the riding phase of AT LEAST 800 points, they may, at the discretion of the Tetrathlon Committee, be invited to compete at the Championships.

b. At Area Competitions: in cases of genuine lameness (certified by either a Veterinary Surgeon or the Official Steward), a competitor shall score zero for the riding phase, but they may, at the discretion of the Tetrathlon Chairman, be invited to compete at the Championships if the combination of horse and rider has demonstrated an appropriate standard of cross country ability in the current year.

c. Out of Area requests from Open, Intermediate and Junior competitors can only be made by the Area Representative to the Tetrathlon Committee, with a copy to The Tetrathlon Secretary. In order to qualify out of Area a competitor must have achieved a minimum ride score of 800 points. Qualifying Members may join their Branch/ Centre Team at the Championships, assuming the team qualifies.

d. Low riding scores: In the interests of safety, competitors must achieve a minimum riding score of 800 points at their Area competition in order to qualify for the Championships. The Official Steward may make a recommendation to the Tetrathlon Chairman that this Rule should be waived in certain circumstances, and that an invitation to the Championships be extended to the competitor.

e. A competitor who misses the Area Competition because they are a Member of an Official Pony Club team competing overseas may be invited to compete at the Tetrathlon Championships as an individual. If two Individuals from their own Branch/Centre qualify for the Championships, they may join them to make up a team of three.

f.   Mixed Teams

Mixed Teams cannot consist of more than two of each gender, and members may not be a part of any other team. Mixed Teams may qualify for the Championships at their Area competition.

g.   Area Teams

Individual Members from the same Area who qualify at an Area competition, but are not in any other team, may be declared to form an Area Team at the Championships. **Each Area can declare one Open, one Intermediate and one Junior team.**

Declarations must be submitted in writing to the Secretary by the Area Tetrathlon Co–ordinator or other designated person by 9.00am on the first day of the Championship competition.

h.   Mixed Branch Teams

If a Branch/Centre is unable to field a Team, they may combine with another Branch/Centre in a similar situation to form a Team to compete at the Area Competition, but they are not eligible to qualify for the Championships. Individual Members of the Team may qualify for the Championships as Individuals.

51.   THE CHAMPIONSHIPS

a.   The Championships consist of:

- ▸ THE OPEN TEAM COMPETITION

- ▸ THE OPEN INDIVIDUAL COMPETITION

- ▸ THE OPEN MIXED GENDER TEAM COMPETITION

- ▸ THE INTERMEDIATE TEAM COMPETITION

- ▸ THE INTERMEDIATE INDIVIDUAL COMPETITION

- ▸ THE INTERMEDIATE MIXED GENDER TEAM COMPETITION

- ▸ THE JUNIOR TEAM COMPETITION

- ▸ THE JUNIOR INDIVIDUAL COMPETITION

- ▸ THE JUNIOR MIXED GENDER TEAM COMPETITION

- ▸ MIXED AREA TEAMS

b. **Awards**

Rosettes and Salvers will be awarded. Best run/swim/shoot will be awarded a Championship trophy and all competitors will be awarded a Championship medal.

GOLD, SILVER and BRONZE AWARDS

Open Boys and Girls:

▸ **Gold**
4250 & 1400 ride
▸ **Silver**
4100 & 1350 ride
▸ **Bronze**
3900 & 1301 ride

52.   ENTRIES

a.   **Area Competitions** – Entries should be sent, together with an entry fee to the Secretary of the organising Branch/Centre. Details are to be found in the competition schedule. Entry fees should be set at a reasonable level by the Organiser in order to cover competition costs. A start fee may be charged if necessary.

b.   **Championships**

i.   Entries for competitors who have qualified for the Championships, should be made via the online Entry system as per the competition schedule.
ii.   Teams or Individuals qualifying for the Championships but not wishing to go forward must inform the Organiser before Area prize giving so that the qualification can be passed to the next highest placed team.
iii.   Immediately following Area Competitions the Area Representative may invite qualifying individuals who are not in any Branch Team to form one Open, **one Intermediate, and one Junior** Area Team of any combination of Boys or Girls. At the competition, they must inform the Organiser of the Area Competition, or Secretary of the Championships, in writing, of the name of the person appointed to be their representative.

53.   WITHDRAWAL (FOR ALL COMPETITIONS)

If a Branch or Centre withdraws a team or individual prior to the closing date for a competition, a full refund of entry and stabling fees will be made, less an administration charge. Withdrawals after the closing date for a competition will not be refunded.

54.   ABANDONMENT (FOR ALL COMPETITIONS)

In the event of a competition being abandoned, for whatever reason, a refund of 50% of the entry fee will be given. In such an instance the refund process will be communicated and must be followed.

55.   SUBSTITUTION

a.   Area Competitions

After the closing date for declarations no substitutions may be made of horses or riders except in cases of illness, lameness or other unavoidable circumstance, which must be certified by the District Commissioner, Centre Proprietor or appointed representative.

In such a case:

i.   If a horse has to be substituted an alternative competitor may be nominated.

ii.   If a competitor has to be substituted an alternative horse may be nominated.

iii.   If a Branch/Centre enters two teams substitution may be made from one team to the other.

b.   The Championships

i.   **Teams –** No substitutions may be made of horses or competitors except in the case of illness, lameness or other unavoidable circumstance, which must be certified by The District Commissioner/Centre Proprietor. In such a case, if a horse has to be substituted an alternative rider may be nominated, and if a rider has to be substituted an alternative horse may be nominated.

ii.   **Individuals –** A substitute horse may be entered only in the case of illness, lameness or other unavoidable circumstance, which must be certified by the District Commissioner/Centre Proprietor. Riders may not be substituted.

iii.   All substituted Members must have competed at the Area Competition and have achieved a minimum ride score of 800 points. Substitute horses must meet the defined Championship eligibility criteria.

At both Area Competitions and the Championships

    i.   No rider may be substituted after the competition has started.

    ii.   No horse may be substituted after the Riding Phase has started.

    iii.   No horse or competitor replaced by a substitute may re–enter the competition.

    iv.   In all cases of substitution the District Commissioner, Centre Proprietor or appointed representative must certify in writing that the substitute is eligible.

d.   Should qualified teams/individuals be unable to compete at the Championships the next competitor/team down could compete providing the substitution was made 7 days before the Championships.

e.   All Members and substitutes competing at the Championships must have competed in all four phases of the Area Competition.

56.   BRANCH/CENTRE REPRESENTATIVE

If the District Commissioner or Centre Proprietor of a competing team or individual is unable to be present at the competition, they must inform the Organiser of the Area Competition, or Secretary of the Championships, in writing, of the name of the person appointed to be their representative.

PART 4 – NOTES FOR ORGANISERS

These notes are written for the guidance of those involved in running Tetrathlon competitions. They are not exhaustive and there are alternative ways of running particular phases which are as good. It is also possible to run this type of competition on a local and informal basis with fewer Officials than suggested here. However, any drastic pruning of Officials in any competition where there is a serious rivalry between teams or individuals is apt to lead to a deluge of protests.

N.1   TIMINGS

Although a considerable physical challenge, it is perfectly feasible to run a Tetrathlon competition in one day.

a.   The first phase, where possible, should be the shooting, while the competitors hands are steady, followed by one of the strenuous dismounted phases (swimming or running). Next should come the riding and finally the other dismounted phase. For ease of scoring and producing the results, it is usually best to finish with the running.

b.   Suggested timings for a competition with 40–50 entries are as follows:

- **Shooting:** (9.30am–12.30pm) Four targets, 15 minutes per detail (a time of 12 minutes may be feasible, but there are often delays which might upset such a tight schedule).
- **Swimming:** 12.00pm–1.30pm Four lanes, 7 minutes per detail. Riding: 2.00pm–3.30pm Competitors ideally at not less than 2 minute intervals.
- **Running:** 4.00pm–4.45pm Competitors at 1 minute intervals.
- **Prize giving:** 5.30pm

c.   The above timings make a very long and strenuous day, but with that number of competitors it is the minimum consistent with giving everybody time to prepare themselves and walk the running and riding courses before they compete. For the senior competitors, who do longer distances, it is also a considerable strain, and it is better to hold the competition over two days.

d.   In a two–day competition, if possible, one of the strenuous dismounted phases should be on the first day and the other, together with the riding, on the second. Shooting should be the first item on one of the days and this will often be possible where there is an urban sports complex for the swimming.

e.　　Timings will often be governed by the period when a swimming pool can be booked.

N.2　ORDER OF STARTING

The order in which the competitors start on the various phases needs careful consideration, especially in a one–day competition.

a.　　When time is tight in a one–day competition, it is only fair that the same order should be adhered to throughout, otherwise a competitor late in the order may find themself going straight from one phase to another without time for walking the course, warming up, food, etc.

b.　　In the shooting, since Members may well be using the same pistol or coach/loader, they should follow each other in successive details at the same stand.

c.　　In the riding phase of a Branch/Centre event where horses may be shared, the order may have to be completely altered to allow shared horses to go early and late. In a tight one–day event this phase may well dictate the whole order.

N.3　ORGANISATION

a.　　If the competition takes place on one day, it is not possible for one person to control all the phases, as some of them will have to be set up and started before the preceding phase has finished. On two days it is just possible, provided entries do not exceed about 50, but the Organiser will be very stretched.

b.　　It is far better, and in Area competitions essential, to delegate the control and organisation of each of the four phases to separate Phase Stewards. The Organiser exercises general control, deciding any general disputes and, in particular, controlling the scoring team. With an adequate team of Officials it is possible to handle at least 100 competitors. Over a 2 day competition it is possible to handle more competitors.

c.　　It is important that anyone organising a Tetrathlon recruits a really good scoring team. It is vitally important that the scorers are protected from the attention of competitors, trainers and parents. If at the end of a competition teams have to wait a long time for results, and when they do come they are inaccurate, a competition which may have run smoothly can end in discord.

d.　　In accordance with The Pony Club Health and Safety Rule Book, the Organiser or a representative must carry out an inspection of the competition site prior to the competition and complete a Pony Club risk assessment and emergency planning check list. Templates for risk assessments and emergency planning can be found on The Pony Club website or by contacting The Pony Club Office.

N.4   PERSONNEL

The principal officials needed to organise a Tetrathlon competition are:

- ▶ Organiser
- ▶ Pony Club Official Steward (Official Events only)
- ▶ Secretary and/or Assistant Organiser
- ▶ Chief Steward for each phase
- ▶ Chief Scorer and three scorers
- ▶ Three runners

The organiser is in overall control; unless there is an Official Steward who heads the Jury of Appeal for protests and briefs stewards and Judges where appropriate. The organiser, and the Phase Stewards, must avoid involving themselves in specific tasks. They should remain free and able to deal with any problems that arise. The secretary takes the entries and attends to all the paperwork, finance, etc., before, during and after the competition. The runners take results, as they are written down by the judges for various phases, to the scoring team (separate messengers or gallopers are needed for the riding.

N.5   PROGRAMME

A programme may be provided for sale to spectators and competitors. The sports sponsor's name should be included in the heading. It should give each competitor's number, forename and surname, age (on the day of the Competition), Branch/Centre, name of horse. Columns for writing down the scores are appreciated by spectators. The names of the Official Steward, Organiser, Phase Stewards and the Jury of Appeal should also be given.

It is advisable to print a note in your programme reminding spectators of the Forbidden Assistance rules. Additional space, if any, might well be devoted to a brief description of Tetrathlon, the names of other Officials and an outline of the work of The Pony Club. The date and venue of the Championships is also appreciated.

Advertisements from local firms can provide a source of revenue, provided they are not directly in competition with the sport sponsor. If you have any concerns about sponsorship please contact The Pony Club Office.

RIDING PHASE

N.6   THE COURSE

a.   Planning and Construction

When planning and constructing a Tetrathlon riding course the aim is to test the rider and not the horse. If a British Eventing course is to be used, the addition of portable fences can be put to good use to alter the course to suit Tetrathlon requirements. The fences should be solid, strong and inviting.

b.   Alternative 'L' Obstacles

The primary purpose of an Alternative 'L' Obstacle is to assist in the training and encouragement of inexperienced riders, to give them every chance to complete the course. There shall be a minimum of 3 'L' obstacles, providing an easy alternative to the more difficult obstacles of the Riding Phase (excluding gate and slip rail). These Alternative 'L' Obstacles may consist of only one easy element, which may present an alternative to a single or a multiple main obstacle. The ability of the course designer/Official Steward to assess the obstacles most likely to require an Alternative 'L' Obstacle may prove an important factor in the outcome of the Riding Phase. The Alternative 'L' Obstacle must therefore present essentially minimum difficulty to the rider, at preferably all difficult obstacles.

c.   Marking the Course

The course should be marked adequately with direction indicators wherever, after negotiating an obstacle, the route to the next is not obvious.

d.   Practice Jumps

A practice jump(s) should be provided near the start, marked with red and white flags.

N.7   GATE AND SLIP RAIL

The gate should be hung so that it only opens in one direction of travel, where possible, in the direction of travel of horse and rider, and is reasonably easy to open and shut providing the rider takes it correctly (facing their horse the right way, making it move sideways, etc.). The latch should be designed so that it can be unfastened, and the gate opened with one hand. A gate that shuts and latches itself when left untouched is an inadequate test. The latch must be robust enough to withstand repeated use. A wire loop is not really robust enough; a rope loop is a good substitute. If the gate and slip rail are not in an existing fence, a length of fencing must be constructed, extending at least 3 metres on either side. The gate should open in one direction only and where possible, in the direction of travel of horse and rider. **No more than one slip rail should be available for competitors to use.**

a.   Siting

These obstacles should not be sited too early in the course, and before horses are going freely. One of them at about fence 4-6 makes a convenient mark on the course for despatching the next rider. It may also be a good thing to site one or both in such a way that a rider going fast needs to 'take a pull' if they are to negotiate the obstacle efficiently.

b.   Design

    i.   The gate should be hung so that it only opens in one direction and is reasonably easy to open and shut providing the rider takes it correctly (facing their horse the right way, making it move sideways, etc.). The latch should be designed so that it can be unfastened and the gate opened with one hand. A gate that shuts and latches itself when left untouched is an inadequate test. The latch must be robust enough to withstand repeated use. A wire loop is not really robust enough; a rope loop is a good substitute.

    ii.   The slip rail must not be too heavy for a small rider to lift.

c.   Flagging/Marking

The gate that is to be opened and the slip rail that is to be taken down must be clearly flagged on the ground and marked on any plan of the course that is exhibited. Especially as it is quite common to have similar looking obstacles which the rider is required to jump.

d.   Air Jackets

The riding phase can include a sign before and after the Slip rail to remind riders of the need to 'unclip air jacket' and 're–clip air jacket' to prevent them from accidentally going off when dismounting for the slip rail. These signs are not forbidden assistance as they will be there for each rider whether they are wearing an air jacket or not.

e.   Judging

The rules for judging and scoring the gate and slip rail are complicated. The Judges should be selected with this in mind and specially briefed. Besides the Judge at these obstacles, an extra official is necessary at each with a separate stop–watch for timing a competitor who is held up by the one in front.

N.8   BRIEFING

a.   Fence Judges

Special attention must be paid to the briefing of Fence Judges. Apart from the peculiarities of the gate and slip rail, all will need to appreciate the differences from Eventing. The main ones are that the scoring for refusals, falls, etc., though having the same pattern, is on a much greater scale (in order to make it comparable with other phases). At the gate and slip rail there are also circumstances when the Fence Judge must give information, instructions or assistance to the competitor.

b.   Forbidden Assistance

It is important to ensure that Judges, competitors, parents and other supporters are fully aware of the rules concerning Forbidden Assistance. A briefing session for competitors and supporters may be necessary for this, among other purposes, but other means should be used if possible because such a session may disrupt their crowded programme.

N.9   RUN–IN

The run–in from the last fence should be short.

N.10   OFFICIALS

a.   Required Officials

The organisation for the riding phase is similar to that of a hunter trial or Cross Country phase of Eventing. The following team of officials is required:

- Health and Safety Steward
- Collecting Ring Steward(s)
- Fence Judges (and hazard)*
- Starter
- Timekeepers (two)

*A compulsory turning point on the Course should be monitored either by a fence Judge or by a separate Judge.

While it is the responsibility of competitors to ensure that their saddlery and dress are correct in accordance with the Rules it is advisable to appoint an official to do checks.

b.   Medical and Veterinary

Please refer to The Pony Club Health and Safety, Safeguarding and Horse

Welfare Rule Book.

c.   Communications

   i.   Medical personnel, the Veterinary Surgeon and the Ambulance are best sited near control.

   ii.   Organisers must ensure that the communication system, whether by radio or flags, is such that an accident at any fence can be notified to control as quickly as possible.

   iii. Routes around the course for medical personnel with an Ambulance and for the Veterinary Surgeon must be reconnoitred in advance.

N.11   JUDGING

a.   If using older fence Judges, it is advisable to pair them with a younger, active person (Must be between 18-75 years of age).

b.   Each fence Judge must be provided with clipboard, or a board with a bulldog clip, and a pencil, Pony Club Tetrathlon Riding Score Sheet (Individual obstacle) or Pony Club Tetrathlon Riding Score Sheet (Gate and Slip Rail), and timetable of competitors starting times. A copy of the leaflet 'Notes for briefing Fence Judges and Fence Judge Instructions' should be sent to Fence Judges several days in advance.

c.   All Judges should have some kind of time–piece (ideally a stop–watch) to record the time each rider jumps their fence and the time a rider is held up at their fence through no fault of their own.

d.   Judges should enter up all their sheets with their name, fence number and sheet number, but it is important that no rider's number is entered until they appear at the approach to the obstacle, and this point should be emphasised at the briefing.

e.   Faults should be entered in the appropriate columns, but it is better that they should not be totalled. If a rider negotiates the obstacle without penalty, the Fence Judge puts a tick in the Remarks column. Fence Judges should check the completion of each sheet before they hand it to the score collector, retaining the counterfoil in their score pad.

N.12   STARTING

a.   Riders should report to the collecting ring some minutes before their scheduled time. Here the Collecting Ring Steward checks their dress and saddlery and sends them in turn to the start.

b.   The rider should be started at a suitable moment, at approximately the scheduled time. Since there is no requirement to start at an exact moment on the clock, a countdown is not compulsory.

N.13   TIME KEEPING

Stop watches/chronometers must be synchronised. There should always be at least one spare, which is running and synchronized, at the start and finish. Starting and finishing times are recorded for every rider. The time taken is obtained by subtracting the starting time from the finishing time.

N.14   JUDGES' FLAGS

The colours for signalling flags shall be:

- **RED**
  First Aid (Ambulance and Doctor)
- **BLUE**
  Veterinary Surgeon
- **WHITE**
  Fence Repair
- **RED FLAG WAVED AT WAIST HEIGHT IN FRONT OF THE COMPETITOR**
  Stop
- **ALL THREE FLAGS WAVED TOGETHER TOWARDS CONTROL**
  Delay the start of further competitors

N.15   MESSENGERS

Can be Pony Club Members or adults mounted on horses or ponies. ATVs / Cross Country Motorbikes are often used; the driver must be at least 17yrs old, highly responsible and wearing the appropriate headgear.

The Steward in charge of score collection should be an adult and must ensure that everyone knows their way around the Cross Country course, which fences are their responsibility, not forgetting the timekeepers' score sheets and to where the score sheets should be taken thus keeping the scorers supplied with up to date information.

The success of a well run competition relies on information being given to the scorers as quickly and efficiently as possible.

N.16   ALL-TERRAIN VEHICLES* AND MOTOR CYCLES

The use of ATVs, quad bikes and motorcycles poses significant risks. Prior permission from the organiser must be obtained before using any of these vehicles.

Any use must be documented in a specific risk assessment and these guidelines must be followed:

- ▸ Drivers must be aged 17 years or over (unless especially agreed with the Insurers)
- ▸ Helmets must be worn
- ▸ Drivers must have received adequate training for the vehicle they are driving (ensure this is recorded and signed by the trainer and participant)
- ▸ Only vehicles designed to carry passengers should be used for this purpose
- ▸ Vehicles should be maintained in good condition

The Pony Club Public Liability Insurance provides indemnity to The Pony Club in respect of legal liability for injury or damage, provided the above guidelines are followed. However, this insurance only comes into effect if there is no other insurance in force which could provide cover. Owners of motor cycles requiring compulsory insurance under the Road Traffic Acts should note that claims involving their motor cycles would fall under their individual policies. It is recommended that such owners advise their insurer of the use of their motor cycle at events.

HEALTH, SAFETY AND WELFARE GUIDELINES

a. Only Event Officials who have received proper training, hold current appropriate licences, have no serious convictions, have a reasonable accident record and are aged 17 or over (unless especially agreed by Underwriters) should drive/ride these machines.

b. Passengers should not be carried unless the vehicle is designed or adapted for that purpose except in an emergency. Drivers, riders and passengers MUST wear suitable safety headwear.

c. The vehicles should be roadworthy and maintained in good condition and are only to be used for purposes directly connected with the Event.

d. If machines travel on or across a public road, motor insurance is compulsory.

e. The Pony Club Public Liability Insurance provides indemnity to The Pony Club in respect of legal liability for injury or damage if negligence of The Pony Club is proven, provided the above guidelines are followed. However, this insurance only comes into effect if compulsory insurance is not required and there is no other insurance in force which could provide cover. Owners of motor cycles requiring compulsory insurance under the

Acts should note that claims involving their motor cycles would fall under their individual policies. It is recommended that such owners advise their Insurer of the use at Events.

*Such machines need expert handling as they are inherently unstable.

N.17   JUNIOR AND MINIMUS COMPETITIONS

Particularly in Junior and Minimus Events, the aim is to encourage competitors, not to alarm them; the riding obstacles should be built with this in mind. Provided that it is properly explained on the entry form or schedule, it is quite acceptable in these competitions for Organisers to introduce a rule allowing three refusals at a (specified) number of fences before a rider must retire.

N.18   FRANGIBLE FENCES AND MIMS CLIPS

Frangible Pins

If the Cross Country course incorporates Frangible Pins then the following guidelines should be useful: British Eventing Technical Advisors, or their appointed representative, are responsible for ensuring the pins are correctly fitted. Technical Advisors, or their appointed representative, are also responsible for ensuring the pins are adequately monitored on day of competition, and through fence Judges and course builders, that they are replaced when they need to be – i.e. if a pin bends or breaks. It is therefore important that the British Eventing Technical Advisors or their appointed representative is present on the day if the frangible fence is to be used.

It should be remembered that The Frangible Fence Pin System has been designed to activate under certain circumstances. The version currently in use has been designed in line with the weight of an average horse (470kg).

MIMS Clips

If the course includes a fence with MIMS clips, ensure that there is an accredited course builder there to deal with it should a clip need to be replaced.

It must be stressed that the systems that have been developed are not guaranteed to improve standards of safety and that Cross Country riding remains a risk sport. However the indications are that the Frangible Fence Pin system and MIMS Clip system may minimise the risk of injury to competitors.

RUNNING PHASE

N.19   THE COURSE

a.   It is recommended that the course is measured with a wheel, and that GPS systems are not relied upon as they fail to take account of elevation and are therefore inaccurate.

b.   If the course is in open country it should take advantage of natural ups and downs, but not steep hills, and may include a few permanent obstacles such as gates or rails to surmount. Alternatively, the course may be laid out around fields, sports pitches, or held on an athletics track.

c.   The course should be clearly marked, bearing in mind a tired runner's faculties for looking about them and spotting a flag, and even for going the correct side of it, are impaired.

Where there are compulsory turning points in the course or where a specific route is to be followed (e.g. over an obstacle), red and white boundary markers should be used – flags, posts, etc. Flags are to be placed in such a way that a runner must leave a red flag on their right and a white flag on their left. Such red and white flags or indicators must be respected under penalty of time or retirement wherever they occur on the course. Where necessary, or for greater clarity, a hurdle, tape or string as a 'wing' to prevent runners going the wrong side should be used. Yellow posts, markers or direction arrows should also be used to help runners. If the course is over the same ground as the riding phase, care must be taken to avoid confusion between the different course markers.

N.20   START AND FINISH – Same Point

A good layout is to have the start and finish at the same point, separated by a post (e.g., start on its left, finish on its right). If this is done, good marking of the final stage of the course is essential, preferably with the run–in roped off funnel–wise with rope or tape. It is important that runners' paths do not cross anywhere near the start/ finish, and this area must be kept free of spectators, as when runners finish in a bunch the Judges' job is not easy.

N.21   START AND FINISH – Different Points

The start and finish can be in different places though this is not ideal as extra care must be taken to ensure that the starter's and finish Judge's watches are accurately synchronised.

N.22   OFFICIALS

a.   The following officials are recommended:

▸   Running Steward
▸   Starter and Assistant – who may double as Finish Judge and
    Timekeeper
▸   Scoreboard Writer
▸   Runner(s) – to take result times to the scorers
▸   Course/Turning Point Stewards

b.   At least two watches should be used to avoid disaster from sudden battery run down or from accidentally pressing the stop button. Stop watches which can record several lap or finish times are particularly useful for timing running in heats.

Stewards should be stationed round the course as necessary, to check that the runners complete the course, and that they are not paced by supporters.

N.23   PROCEDURE AND TIMING – TIME TRIALS

a.   Every runner should be started at an exact minute reading on the clock. The easiest way is to start runner No.1 at zero plus one minute, No.2 at two minutes, etc., so that the minutes to be subtracted are the same as the runner's number.

If there is a hold–up, the next runner should be started at the next exact minute. If a scheduled runner is withdrawn, it is advisable to start no–one at that time and adhere to the schedule for the rest of the competitors. If a runner starts other than at their correct minute, this must be noted, so that the time taken can be adjusted as necessary.

b.   The assistant starter acts as collecting ring steward and marshals the runners so that they report to the starter in time and in the correct order.

c.   One minute before the first runner is to start, the starter and time–keeper start their watches simultaneously. The starter warns each runner of the approach of their starting time and starts them by countdown, recording the time of starting (a tick may suffice if he starts at the planned time). They also check that the runner does not cross the line before time, and recalls them if necessary.

d.   It is advisable to have an assistant about 50 metres from the finish calling out each runner's number, as numbers may be difficult to distinguish at the finish on a tired competitor.

e. As each runner comes in, if a split–action watch is not in use, the Judge calls out 'No. (so and so) finishing NOW', whereupon the time–keeper reads the clock and records the reading, together with the runner's number. With a split action time–piece, the time–keeper can of course time a runner's finish directly.

t. The finish Judge checks it as soon as practicable and the scoreboard writer promptly enters the provisional time taken on the board or calls it out for the benefit of spectators – this enables any query to be settled on the spot while the matter is fresh in the Officials' mind.

g. After every five or so runners finish, the time–keeper's record is sent by runner to the scorers. A system may be used of making out a separate 'chit' for each runner, with their start and finish times, which is passed from starter to time–keeper, from them to the writer (who works out provisional time taken) and then passed to the scorers. To guard against loss of chits, a complete record must be retained by the time–keeper.

N.24   PROCEDURE AND TIMING – MASS STARTS

a. Separate heats should be used for different classes. However, when there are a small number of competitors in a class then it may be merged with another class competing over the same distance. When there are a large number of competitors in a class it may be necessary to have more than one heat. Depending on the layout of the course, 12 runners is a maximum heat size.

To enable runners to be placed into seeded heats their anticipated run time should be requested on the entry form. Alternatively the running heats may be composed randomly.

b. The assistant starter acts as collecting ring steward and marshals the runners for the next heat so that they report to the starter in time.

c. For each heat the starter checks the correct runners are at the start line, and informs them of how they will start the race. On the signal to start, all stopwatches are started. If there is a false start the runners are recalled and the heat restarted.

d. As the runners cross the finish line the finish Judge records the competitor numbers in the order in which they finish. It is advisable to have an assistant in case several runners finish together. Also, as each runner finishes the timekeepers record a time for them.

e. When all the runners in a heat have finished, the timekeeper read back the finish times to the finish Judge who records them against the competitor's number. The assistant timekeeper(s) cross checks the recorded times against those from their stopwatch.

f. The finish Judge checks that each competitor has a recorded time. The scoreboard writer then records the time taken on the board or calls it out for the benefit of spectators – this enables any query to be settled on the spot while the matter is fresh in the Officials' mind.

g. Next, the finish Judge's record is sent by runner to the scorers. Alternatively, especially if a mobile phone stopwatch is being used, it may be possible to add the runner numbers against their recorded times and send a text message to the scorers. To guard against loss of data, a complete written record of competitor numbers and finish times must be retained by the finish Judge.

SHOOTING PHASE

N.25 VENUE

a. The shooting phase should take place indoors whenever possible.

b. Apart from purpose–built indoor ranges used by schools, the Armed Forces and shooting clubs, a large barn is often suitable provided there is plenty of light. An indoor riding school is also excellent, providing the lighting is adequate. It is also possible to shoot in village or school halls, provided that adequate precautions are taken to see that pellets do not damage the decor and there can be no ricochet.

c. Lighting

If it is not possible to use natural daylight, the range and targets must be well lit artificially. Care must be taken that either lights or the sun do not shine into the faces of the competitors. For indoor ranges, there should be (as a guide) a minimum of 1000 lux on the targets and 300 lux at the firing point. All targets should be lit evenly. The light conditions must remain equal throughout the shooting competition. If these conditions cannot be met, the Chief Steward should inform Team Officials in advance of shooting.

N.26 THE FIRING POINT

It is essential that those who are on the firing point are physically segregated from spectators and waiting details. Noise should be kept to a minimum whilst shooting is taking place.

N.27　TARGETS

a.　　　The Official Pony Club Target is to be used for all competitions.

b.　　　Mechanical or electrical turning target devices (which alternately face the target to the firer and edge) should be used for Area Competitions if possible. This is particularly desirable in local Open, Intermediate and Junior competitions, otherwise competitors unused to shooting on a turning target may be at a disadvantage when competing at an Area event or at the Championships.

c.　　　Targets must be fixed so that they do not waver or move when hit, or when turned by a device. A backing card of 'Correx' or similar material to which they can be secured by rubber bands is best, but the scoring part of the surface (including the margin) must be kept clear.

d.　Protective Target Backing

If target backings are of hard material (e.g. steel or plastic) they must be angled to ensure that pellets are deflected downwards (and are recommended immediately behind each target).

Absorbent materials such as straw bales, loose (not taut) tarpaulin, blankets or similar materials in layers hung down as a background, will absorb pellets after they have passed through the target. There should not be a hard vertical background immediately behind the targets to avoid danger from ricochet and damage to structures and materials. Should a Kevlar backdrop be utilised, this should have an absorbent dust sheet or blanket hung in front of it, to reduce the incidence of ricochets from the Kevlar.

e.　　　Since each detail takes up to 15 minutes, the more competitors that can be accommodated in one detail the better. Care must be taken to afford competitors enough room to shoot without physical embarrassment from their neighbours, and for their loaders to do their work. As a guide each shooter should have at least 50cm (20") of space at the firing point.

N.28　TABLES

a.　　　A table or bench is to be provided in front of each competitor. A chair may be provided for every firing point located at least 1.5metres (5') behind the firing line.

b.　　　A line, rail, or bar on the floor is needed behind the table as the official distance firing point line (either 7m or 10m). The competitor's feet must remain behind this line during competition.

N.29 SAFETY AND SECURITY

a. The safety of all event participants and spectators requires self–discipline, careful attention to pistol handling, and caution in moving about the range by everybody concerned. It is the responsibility of the competitors (and their loaders if present) to ensure that they load their pistols safely and efficiently. Range safety is the responsibility of all persons in the range environs.

b. An air pistol pellet can cause serious injury to persons at close range. The **Range Conducting Officer** must maintain, as a priority, range safety and ensure the safe handling of pistols at all times. Not only will this help to prevent accidents, but it is also vital training in the safe handling of pistols.

c. In the interest of safety, the **Range Conducting Officer** may stop the shooting at any time.

d. Anyone on the range or in the range environs must immediately notify the **Range Conducting Officer** of any situation that may be dangerous or which may cause an accident.

e. Air pistols must be stored in their cases and locked in a secure place at all times except when on the range. Away from the range pistols should be locked away and secured safely out of sight in a vehicle or alternative secure storage.

f. The shooting range may be accessed only by competitors and officials. Only shooters (and loaders if required) involved in the detail should be at the firing point at any one time on instruction of the **Range Conducting Officer**. An area for spectators should be made available behind the range area and delineated clearly.

g. The **Range Conducting Officer** must enforce strict drills for loading and firing and putting pistols down in a 'safe' condition on the firing point table before anyone moves forward of the firing point. Strict adherence to the instructions regarding Safety and the Words of Command is required.

N.30 OFFICIALS

The following officials are recommended:

▸ Phase Steward
▸ **Range Conducting Officer** and Assistant(s) depending on the number of competitors in each detail. As a guide there should be one official for

no more than 12 targets (Seniors and Intermediate) and no more than 6 targets (Juniors and Minimus)

- ▶ Target Steward(s)
- ▶ Marshalling Steward
- ▶ One Scrutineer/Two Scorers
- ▶ Messenger

The Chief Steward is responsible for supervising the proper conduct of the phase, the smooth running of the event and all appeals.

The **Range Conducting Officer** who is the Chief Range Officer (CRO) is in charge of the shooting range and environs and gives all range commands and instructions. They should not have any other duties such as collecting targets. At larger competitions an official acting as the target operator may also be used, who also acts as an assistant safety officer working under the **Range Conducting Officer**.

The Target Stewards collect/put up the practice and competition targets and take the competition targets and register to the Scorers.

The Scorers and Scrutineer are responsible for the scoring.

The Messenger is available for all errands and for taking the score sheets and scored targets to the competition classification area.

N.31   PROCEDURE

a.   These Rules and Words of Command are to be followed strictly at all times.

b.   The shooting phase is a competition in 'snap shooting' – the essence of which is that the competitor does not know when the target will appear. Care should therefore be taken to observe the interval of approximately 3–4 seconds between either 'Watch and Shoot' and exposure of the targets, or between 'Stand By' and 'Fire' as laid down in the Rules. Operating the range to the correct procedure promotes range safety and ensures equal opportunity for all competitors.

c.   The **Range Conducting Officer** should brief the shooters (and loaders if present) before the start of each detail. Apart from safety matters, the briefing may mention such matters as the procedure for sighting shots/ practice shots, whether fixed or turning targets are in use (if not already notified), the procedure for a target 'dummy run', whether competitors are to put up their own targets and instructions to loaders (if used). Specific Health and Safety instructions particular to the venue should also be included. Each detail should be briefed in exactly the same way. Following the briefing the **Range Conducting Officer** should ask the competitors if there are any questions and respond accordingly. Coaches and spectators may not ask questions.

d.　　　Prior to shooting, all competitors will have to submit to equipment control to check that all are using the correct type and calibre of pistol and ammunition in accordance with these Rules.

e.　　　When turning targets are in use, one target 'dummy run' should be given at the conclusion of the sighting/practice shots. The distinction between the sequence of orders for turning and fixed targets should be noted. With turning targets the order 'Watch and Shoot' means watch the front and shoot when the target appears; no further words are spoken, except in emergency, until the order to reload. With fixed targets the order 'Stand By' takes the place of 'Watch and Shoot', the order 'Fire' takes the place of the appearance of the target after three or four seconds, and the order 'Stop' that of the disappearance of the target.

f.　　　Left handed competitors should be positioned on the far right of the range (or next to an empty lane if possible) so that competitors do not stand face to face on adjacent firing points.

N.32　PUTTING UP AND REMOVING TARGETS

a.　　　For identification purposes the top right hand corner of the practice target should be cut off.

b.　　　The Target Steward collects the completed targets from the frames and hands them to the Scorers for scoring. They must not be shown to any competitor, team official or spectator until they have been officially scored.

c.　　　The target mechanism is to be operated normally by the **Range Conducting Officer**. For manually operated or fixed targets where a stop watch is required, or where the number of competitors dictates, the **Range Conducting Officer** may have an assistant acting as a target operator and additional safety official on the firing point.

d.　　　Competitors or their loaders/helpers may be allowed to put up their own competition targets and to take down their practice ones. The competition targets should be handed immediately to the **Range Conducting Officer** or other nominated official.

e.　　　Appeals on scores by competitors or the team trainers must be settled under supervision of the Chief Steward as soon as possible. Competitors' representatives should only be allowed to remove competition targets from the distribution point once all scores are final and all appeals have been adjudicated.

N.33   SCORING PROCEDURES

a.   All scoring should be conducted by two Scorers and a Scrutineer. They may be separate persons at larger competitions, but in all cases work and compilation of the results should be cross checked and initialled. The Chief Steward should not be the Scrutineer.

The Scorers and Scrutineer should be separated from other competition officials and access to them should be restricted to other officials. They report directly to the Chief Steward.

The following scoring procedures must be double checked by Scorers

   i.   Determining the number of shots on a target
   ii.   Determining the value of individual shots
   iii.   Adding shot values and points to be deducted
   iv.   Adding the individual series and overall total
   v.   Each Scorer must certify his/her work by initialling the target and the Tetrathlon Shooting Score Sheet

b.   **Determining Shot Values**

   i.   Count shots on each target.
   ii.   If apparently less than 5 on any one target look for evidence of extra shots according to the procedure below.
   iii.   Score each shot according to procedure below and record value on reverse of target.
   iv.   Total score values for each target.
   v.   Add two target scores on reverse of second target.
   vi.   Certify your calculations by recognisable signature.
   vii.   Pass to second Scorer for checking and countersigning.
   viii. Any discrepancy in score value, shot count or addition must be passed to the Scrutineer for determination as described below.

All shot holes are scored according to the highest value of any target scoring zone or ring that is hit or touched by that pellet hole. If any part of a higher value scoring ring is touched by a pellet hole, the shot must be scored the higher value of the two scoring zones. This is determined by whether either the pellet hole or a plug or overlay gauge inserted in or over the hole touches any part of the outside edge of the scoring ring.

Shots in dispute must be determined as to value by means of a gauge.

Plug and overlay gauges must always be inserted into or over the shot hole with the target in a horizontal position. The target should be supported in such a way that any plug gauge can be inserted fully into the shot hole whilst not touching any supporting surface. 'Plug gauges with integral magnifier should not be used. 'Eagle Eye' overlay type gauges may be used by the Scorers and Scrutineer.

When the accurate use of the plug gauge is made difficult by the close proximity of another pellet hole, a badly torn pellet hole or overlapping pellet holes, the shot value must be determined by using an overlay gauge of flat, transparent material with an engraved ring of 4.5mm (0.177"). Such a scoring gauge will aid in reconstructing the true position of a pellet hole. The Scorers and Scrutineer may all use an overlay type gauge in arriving at a scoring decision.

A target overlay of flat, transparent material may be helpful to reconstruct the scoring rings on the target when used with a flat overlay gauge or when adjudicating 'skid shots'.

If the two Scorers do not agree on either the value of a shot or number of shots on a target, a decision from the Scrutineer must be requested. The plug gauge may be inserted only once in any single pellet hole and only by the Scrutineer. For this reason the use of a gauge must be marked on the target by the Scrutineer, together with their initials, and showing the result. The value of any shot(s) scored using a plug gauge is final and may not be appealed.

If a plug gauge is used then each Scorer shall examine the target using magnifying equipment as necessary in sequence without conferring. Once each is satisfied they can make a decision then the Scrutineer will ask "Are you satisfied?" Each Scorer will have a '+/– card' and show + (plus) for the higher value and – (minus) for the lower value of shot(s). If cards are not available the thumbs up or down vote may be used. The Scrutineer shall decide the shot value(s) should the Scorers be unable to agree. A competitor, parent or coach/team manager cannot challenge this decision.

The same process shall be used also to determine the number of shots on a target if in doubt and the value of 'skid shots'.

If the target paper is torn or folded back by the pellet either as the target turns or if there is possibly more than one shot in the same hole then the target should be carefully reconstituted before adjudicating the shot(s) value.

Scorers and Scrutineers should examine carefully both sides of the target in cases of doubt to identify possible additional shots in the same hole and when adjudicating 'skid shots'.

Notes on scoring gauges:

Optical gauges such as Eagle Eye should be the first applied to a suspect shot hole. These gauges are magnifying devices, including the recommended Eagle Eye. Some have a very useful shot ring for a 4.5mm pellet hole engraved on the glass.

Overlays are transparent and are useful in determining whether a shot is in or out when the target has close clusters of shots, is torn, or in determining skid shots.

Plug gauges are to be used only as a last resort, and can only be used once per shot hole. When inserted into a crisp hole the gauge shows the exact position of a shot relative to the line.

Double Shot gauges are only really useful in the hands of an experienced scorer and only as a last resort. The gauge can only be used once as it can modify the hole. Most double shots are best determined optically, and triple shots can only be determined optically.

c.   Skid Shots

Shots fired while the target is in motion must not be scored as hits unless the greatest horizontal dimension of the pellet hole (surface pellet marking on the target is ignored) is less than 6.0 mm using an overlay 'skid gauge' of flat, transparent material. If the 'skid shot' hole being 6mm or less touches a higher scoring ring then the shot value shall be the higher score.

All scoring decisions should be marked on the target and initialled by the Scorers including the use of either a plug or 'skid shot' gauge.

The Scorers should enter the scores on the Tetrathlon Scoring Sheet and cross check before passing to the scoring team.

Any decision on number or value of potential multiple shots in one hole or one target will have been adjudicated by the Scorers and Scrutineer and may not be appealed.

Team Officials have the right to appeal the compilation and allocation of the scores and total from each target. They may not appeal the value of any single shot hole in which a plug gauge has been inserted.

No appeals will be accepted after the targets have been checked and signed for. All appeals must be completed on the day of the shooting.

SWIMMING PHASE

N.34   VENUE

a.   A heated swimming pool, outdoor or indoor, should be used if possible, especially for Official Competitions. If an indoor pool can be obtained it makes things easier for Officials, spectators and coaches if the weather is bad.

b.   For local Minimus competitions, an outdoor pool is acceptable, a small private pool being less frightening for those who are not good swimmers.

c.   Public pools and those at schools, etc., can often be booked only at certain times. This may well dictate the order of phases and timings. Organisers should take this into account very early in their planning

N.35   OFFICIALS

The following officials are recommended:

- ▸ Phase Steward
- ▸ Starter/Time–keeper
- ▸ Marshal
- ▸ One Lane Judge per lane
- ▸ Writer
- ▸ Runner

N.36   COMPOSITION OF HEATS

It helps swimmers to give their best performance if swimmers of similar ability are in the same heat. If this is to be done, an estimated swim score should be asked for on the entry form. It is often necessary to produce swim heats first and use the order of competitors as the running order for the other phases.

N.37   PREPARATION OF THE POOL

a.   At least one side of the pool must be marked out for the judging of the distance swum. Modern pools are normally an exact length in metres, usually 25, and should be marked in metres. Older pools should still be marked in metres, the 'metre' at one end being in fact rather greater or less – e.g. in a 100 foot pool, it will be 1.48 metres, in which case alternate complete lengths can be scored as 30 and 31 metres.

b.   Marking

The marking must run in both directions and the marks should be visible, but not necessarily readable, from the opposite side. Chalk has the disadvantage that it washes out if it gets wet. Strips of adhesive tape can be good and, better still, is a continuous length of black tape along the edge of the bath, marked in metres with a different colour for each direction; or, if an enthusiast can be recruited, wooden blocks with a slot in which a card is inserted, with numbers painted on either side (e.g. 8 and 17 metres) are excellent. Or the proprietors of the pool may allow marks to be painted, which is best of all.

c.   Lane Roping

Lane ropes are a must in any serious competition. The management of the pool need prior warning that they are required. If starting blocks are in position, their use by competitors is optional. A stopping rope, for use on a false start, is also necessary, as swimmers hardly ever hear shouts and whistles once in the water. It should be manned by two of the lane Judges.

N.38   SPECTATORS

Many indoor pools have limited gallery space for spectators and limited space round the pool itself. Sometimes it has to be accepted that no spectators can be accommodated at all.

It is important to keep the space around the pool free for officials, competitors and coaches (one per swimmer) otherwise the place becomes so crowded that the officials cannot do their work properly.

N.39   WARM-UP

If there is a separate practice pool, as is found in some major sports complexes, warming up presents no problem, but if not, competitors should be allowed a warm–up swim of a length or more within half an hour of their swim time. If time is tight, it may be necessary to have all the warming up done before the competitive swimming begins. The Phase Steward should organise one or two 'dive only lanes' which are manned by an Official to ensure that Competitors dive and swim forward only. It is the Official's responsibility to ensure competitors swim forwards only and that the diving area is clear before allowing another Competitor into the water.

N.40   THE START

The Phase Steward or the Starter calls out the names of those to swim in the heat and they come to the start. Here they are checked by the Lane Judges, as to the lane number, competitor's number and name (this is advisable since they cannot wear numbers).

The Starter, when they are satisfied the Lane Judges have the swimmers' details, should start the swimmers with a whistle, and a false start is signalled by a second blast on the whistle and the use of a stop rope.

On the start being signalled, the Time–keeper starts their stopwatch. There should be a stand–by watch in use, which may be manned by the Phase Steward.

N.41   THE LANE JUDGES

a.   Lane Judging is an onerous task and requires concentration. During the swim, these Judges keep a record of the complete lengths swum by their respective swimmers, and of the further distance at the end.

Each Judge has a tear–off pad, on which they write the heat number, lane number, swimmer's number and name. During the swim, they make a record each time their swimmer completes a length.

On completion of the first length, he writes a figure 1 with a circle round it (to distinguish it from the other numbers), after the second a 2 with a circle round it, and so on. Thus at the end the total number of complete lengths will appear in the last circle. This is the best way to avoid mistakes which are easy to make if the Judge's attention is distracted.

An additional check is for the lane Judge to enter a vertical arrow indicating which way the competitor was swimming at the finish, the bottom of the page representing the starting end of the bath.

N.B. As a further check on distance swum it may be advisable to have an independent Judge or two noting down the number of lengths each swimmer completes and the direction they were swimming at the end.

b.   The Phase Steward should ensure that someone is appointed to check that the swimmers actually touch the end of the bath each time they turn and that competitors do not walk on the bottom. This can be done by an independent person or by the lane Judges at the Phase Steward's discretion.

N.42   THE FINISH

a.   Signals

The Time–keeper gives the half–time call and calls the countdown (half time and 30 secs). These times may be signalled by ringing a hand bell, swimmers should be warned of its meaning before the start.

The Starter (or Time–keeper, if one person fills both roles) signals the finish with a blast on the whistle.

b. **Countdown**

During the countdown, each lane Judge walks level with their swimmer, stopping exactly when the whistle goes, so that he can read off the further distance swum (in completed metres) by means of the marks along the edges of the pool.

The lane Judges, after recording the odd metres, tear off their sheets and send or take them back to the Writer, who writes the lengths and extra distance on a board which can be seen by the coaches. Any queries on swim results must go through the Phase Steward.

Finally, lane Judges' sheets, or a consolidated record of the heat, are taken to the Scorers by the runner.

N.43   TIMINGS

Provided a good drill has been thought out and is followed, there should be no difficulty in running the swimming smoothly. Four–minute swims can be completed comfortably in seven or eight minutes per heat (and three–minute in a minute less). It can be done quicker, but at risk of confusion and error or of unnecessary pressure on competitors.

N.44   SWIM ENGLAND ADVICE TO COMPETITION ORGANISERS

a.   **Before the Competition:**

Carry out a risk assessment and emergency plan for the facility and event organisation.

i.   Check the pool water depth at each end of the pool; remember diving should not take place into water less than 1.35 metres under any circumstances. A water depth of 1.35m minimum is required, extending from 1.0m to at least 6.0m from the wall where the diving will take place.

ii.   If the height of the pool edge is not more than 0.40 metres above the level of water, **and there is a minimum water depth of 1.50 metres**, swimmers that have achieved the Preliminary Competitive Start Award/Swimming Teachers Association Competitive Starts & Turns Level 1 may dive from poolside/**blocks**.

iii.   If the height of the starting blocks is not more than 0.75 metres

above the level of the water, **and there is a minimum water dept**
of 1.35 metres, swimmers that have achieved the Competitive
Start Award /Swimming Teachers Association Competitive Starts &
Turns Level 2 may dive off from **poolside/blocks**.

b.   At the start of the Competition:

Competitors should be notified of:

i.   The pool water depth at each end of the pool. If the water depth is
less than 0.9m then tumble turns should be prohibited.
ii.   The use of starting blocks and the depth of the pool at that point.
iii.   The fact that ASA Laws permits a competitor to start/takeover
in the water, with a dive from the poolside or with a dive from a
starting block.

**c.   At the Competition and at the start of each subsequent
session:**

i.   The referee is in complete control of the competition
ii.   There should be sufficient officials to control the event, particularly
the warm–up session.
iii.   The depth of the pool water at entry should be announced before
each warm up.
iv.   In the event of a false start no swimmers are to 'topple' into the
water – a proper shallow dive should be performed.

d.   Lifesaver

A lifeguard must be present at all Pony Club events (Training and
Competitions). The lifeguard must have an up to date recognized
lifeguarding qualification with an up to date first aid at work qualification.

N.45   ORGANISATION OF BRANCH/CENTRE
COMPETITIONS

In these competitions the rules may be modified at the discretion of
the Organiser, Area Representative, or Tetrathlon Coordinator if local
conditions warrant it. While in official Area Competitions the design of
the riding phase should be similar to that which competitors will meet in
the Championships, it is recommended that in informal Branch/Centre
events the course should present less difficult problems. Lower maximum
dimensions may enable the less experienced riders or horses to negotiate it
without excessive retirements.

N.46 BIATHLONS AND TRIATHLONS

These can be organised at in conjunction with Hunter trials and even one–day events, where competitors only wish to take part in the Cross Country phase. The usual event to leave out is the Swimming, owing to the weather and the likelihood that there is no suitable swimming pool close by.

Members can also qualify to take place in the Winter Triathlon Championship. Areas hold qualifying competitions consisting of the run, swim and shoot phases throughout the winter months and the Championship is held in the spring.

See Appendix D for further details on the Winter Triathlon.

PART 5 – SCORING IN THE TETRATHLON

N.47   GENERAL

a.   The production of quick and accurate scores, kept up to date with running totals as the phases progress, adds greatly to the interest and is vital to the general success of the event.

b.   Long delays at the end of an event, when members/parents/ Guardians/trainers want to get their horses and themselves home, are most unpopular. If the riding is the last phase, producing the results promptly and without mistakes needs good organisation and capable workers. For this reason, it is usually preferable to have the running or swimming last; but some feel that the riding, as the principal feature of any Pony Club Event, should have pride of place as the deciding phase.

c.   It is important to emphasise the division of responsibility between the Judges, Timekeepers, etc. of a phase, and the Scorers.

The Judges and timekeepers produce the factual statistics of the phase, (i.e. distances, times, faults, etc. of each competitor) and it is the Scorers' job to turn these into marks and scores. The factual results may be sent to a central scoring place, or the scorers for a particular phase may be detached to work alongside the Judges. Whatever system is used, it is vital for accurate results to keep this division.

d.   All Scorers' work should be subject to an independent check, as it is too easy, particularly in the latter stages of a competition, for scorers to make mistakes either in their arithmetic or on transferring an item from one form to another. This independent check is best done by two scorers working out the results separately and not comparing their figures until the end of an operation.

e.   Preliminary scores in each phase should be displayed on site as soon as possible, in order that queries may be settled.

f.   Scorers must not be involved in any avoidable calculation on the spot. All conversion of times and distances into scores and penalties should be done by the means of ready reckoners tables prepared beforehand. The scorer simply reads off the score (or riding time penalties) against the performance reported by the Judges.

N.48   OFFICIALS

a.　　The scoring team should consist of a Chief Scorer and three scorers. A fourth scorer should be added at times of pressure, so they can work in pairs leaving the Chief Scorer to exercise general supervision. A separate Official to keep the public scoreboard written up is also useful.

b.　　It is said that good scorers are a particular breed. They do need to be conscientious people, possess stamina, to be able to concentrate independently on the job, and be reasonably good and quick at figures.

c.　　The Scorers must never be involved personally with any of the competitors or teams.

N.49   DEPLOYMENT

a.　　The scoring team should have an office, completely on their own and isolated from the public; a caravan is very suitable. No–one except the scorers, the messengers bringing results from Judges, the Organiser or their assistant, the Official Steward where applicable, and Phase Stewards, should be allowed into the office.

b.　　The scoring office can be moved from place to place if the venues of the phases necessitate it, but unnecessary movement is not desirable as it disrupts the scorers' concentration and is not helpful to accurate work.

c.　　All queries by team managers or competitors must be channelled through the Organiser or their assistant, who can then discuss the query with the Chief Scorer at an opportune moment, and give a decision or the information requested.

N.50   FORMS AND SCORE SHEETS

a.   Dismounted Phases

These are quite simple, their purpose being to record the Judges' reports and the points scored.

b.   Riding Phase

The Tetrathlon Riding Score Sheets (individual obstacle or gate and slip rail) should be used and are available from The Pony Club Office. The normal Eventing Cross Country master score sheet is entirely suitable for Tetrathlon riding phase. In the last line of the form, instead of Scorers' initials, should be entered the rider's final score, i.e. 1400 minus the total penalty points.

c. Consolidated Score Sheet

The scores in the various phases have to be entered on a consolidated score sheet, shown below. This has columns for each phase and, after the second, third and last phases, for the totals of phases to date. Columns are also needed for individual placings, team scores and team placings.

The nature of each phase (shoot, swim, etc.) should be entered in the headings below (1st Phase) etc. (see example below)

The Pony Club Tetrathlon Consolidated Results

Branch	No.	Name	Age	1st Phase	2nd Phase	Score After 2 Phases

3rd Phase	Score After 3 Phases	4th Phase	Total Score	Place	Team Score	Place

d. Public Scoreboard

The public scoreboard should be similarly designed. In the riding scores the symbols D, R, W should be used where appropriate, the figure 0 being reserved for the case where the total penalties add up to 1400 or more. It is preferable in the riding phase to show the riding faults, time faults and score in separate columns on the public scoreboard, if possible.

N.51 CONDUCTING SCORING

a. One way of conducting the scoring (assuming the event starts with the shooting) is for a pair of scorers to be sent to the range, where they make out the shooting score sheets, sending them from time to time to the office. Meanwhile the other two scorers prepare the consolidated score sheet and the public scoreboard from the entries confirmed by the Secretary.

b. As opportunity offers, the scorers in the office enter up the scores from the shooting forms onto the consolidated sheet, checking each other's work. If the next phase does not overlap the shooting, the pair there can move on to it (e.g. swimming) and enter up the relevant form, sending it from time to time to the office, where the scores are entered as before. If there is an overlap, the forms from the second phase must be sent by messenger direct to the office; the two scorers there process them and enter the scores on the chart, as well as dealing with the shooting scores as they come in. The shooting scorers can join the others at the office when the shooting is finished, or go on to yet another dismounted phase if it too overlaps the second.

c.   The scorers left in the office also enter the aggregate scores of phases to date. This not only enhances the interest of competitors and supporters, it also speeds the work at the end, since only two figures have to be added, the checked total of three phases and the scores in the last phase, instead of all four phase scores.

d.   For the riding all scorers remain concentrated in the office and an extra hand or two may be needed, since there are time penalties, as well as the many fence–judging sheets, to be handled.

All these are entered on the riding Master Sheet and the total riding scores found and transferred to the chart. If the riding is the last phase, this is when the pressure is on, since the compilation of riding scores and the production of total scores for the event have to go on simultaneously. The Chief Scorer should keep out of the detailed work at this stage, leaving them free to supervise the whole team and deal with queries both from their own scorers and, possibly, competitors or team managers; as long as the Organiser is involved and happy for the Chief scorer to deal with such matters.

APPENDICES

APPENDIX A - READY RECKONERS

1. Ready reckoners are provided and should be used to convert

Judge's output into scores. Failure to use them leads to mistakes and slow scoring.

2. Ready reckoners for Open, Intermediate, Junior and Minimus Triathlon Run and Swim (25 metre pool) are in this Appendix. Ride time penalties and Swims other than in a 25 metre pool require specific ready reckoners tailored to the length of the course and the pool respectively.

3. Ready reckoners provide specific time penalties or positive scores for every outcome reported by the Judge. The ready reckoner shows the Run score or Ride time penalty against the time taken and the Swim score against the completed lengths and metres reported.

4. Constructing a ready reckoner is simple and is undertaken by all Eventing scorers. After arranging suitable columns for whole minutes or whole lengths and setting out the 60 seconds or the appropriate further metres (according to the length of the pool), start at a suitable known score and enter each one successively after that.

5. Thus in the example of riding time faults, with a time allowed of 4 minutes 45 seconds, start at that time and enter 0 against it. Then against each further second, enter successively 2, 4, 6, 8 etc., until reaching the maximum time penalties considered worth providing for.

6. Human error is as inevitable in this as in any other arithmetical process, so checks must be made. Calculate various scores at random and check that the reckoner agrees. Ensure that the difference between figures in adjacent columns is correct, e.g. that the difference between 5 minutes 50 seconds and 6 minutes 50 seconds in the Riding is 2 x 60 = 120 points. Ensure, of course, that all riding time faults are even numbers.

N.B. Any number whose digits add up to a multiple of 3 is itself such a multiple)

7. Pools whose length is an exact number of metres present no problem, but some are of lengths such as 30 yards or 100 feet. The solution recommended is to mark out the pool in metres from the starting end and take up any incomplete metre in the ready reckoner 100 ft. for instance, is 30.48 metres, virtually 30.5. In this case the side is marked up to 29 metres from the starting end and on completing one length the swimmer scores for 30 metres; on turning and passing the first 'metre' mark, they have done 30.5 plus 1.5, or 32 metres, and scores accordingly, and so on for every alternative length. (Changes in scale of scoring are in bold.)

Much the same can be done with 30 yards, which is 27.43 metres, putting out 26 metre marks. No substantial inaccuracy arises from treating a 25–yard pool (22.86 m) as exactly 23 m. No attempt should be made to score in fractions of a metre; all distances not measured in whole metres in the first place should be rounded off to the nearest whole metre.

8. Before using an example from this Appendix, or an old or borrowed reckoner, check to make sure that it is based on the scale of scoring that appears on the schedule of the event. A reckoner made for some past event at 4 points each for the first 100 metres is useless for one in which 4 points are to be scored for the first 50.

EXAMPLE OF READY RECKONER FOR TIME FAULTS IN RIDING AT 2 PENALTIES PER COMPLETED SECOND OVER TIME ALLOWED

This example is for a course with Time Allowed of 4 min. 45 secs. (including the 60 sec. extra for gate and slip rail). For any other Time Allowed, a ready reckoner must be constructed on similar lines.

secs.	4 min pts.	5 min pts.	6 min pts.	7 min pts.
0		30	1 50	270
1		32	1 52	272
2		34	1 54	274
3		36	1 56	276
4		38	1 58	278
5		40	1 60	280
6		42	1 62	282
7		44	1 64	284
8		46	1 66	286
9		48	1 68	288
10		50	1 70	290
11		52	1 72	292
12		54	1 74	294
13		56	1 76	296
14		58	1 78	298
15		60	1 80	300
16		62	1 82	302
17		64	1 84	304
18		66	1 86	306
19		68	1 88	308
20		70	1 90	31 0
21		72	1 92	31 2
22		74	1 94	31 4
23		76	1 96	31 6
24		78	1 98	31 8
25		80	200	320
26		82	202	322
27		84	204	324
28		86	206	326
29		88	208	328
30		90	210	330
31		92	21 2	332
32		94	21 4	334
33		96	21 6	336
34		98	21 8	338
35		1 00	220	340
36		1 02	222	342
37		1 04	224	344
38		1 06	226	346
39		1 08	228	348
40		11 0	230	350
41		11 2	232	352
42		11 4	234	354
43		11 6	236	356
44		11 8	238	358
45	0	1 20	240	360
46	2	1 22	242	362
47	4	1 24	244	364
48	6	1 26	246	366
49	8	1 28	248	368
50	1 0	1 30	250	370
51	1 2	1 32	252	372
52	1 4	1 34	254	374
53	1 6	1 36	256	376
54	1 8	1 38	258	378
55	20	1 40	260	380
56	22	1 42	262	382
57	24	1 44	264	384
58	26	1 46	266	386
59	28	1 48	268	388

TETRATHLON OPEN BOYS SWIMMING

Ready Reckoner for 25 metre pool

1000 points for 11 Lengths 10 Metres +/- 3 points per Metre

Lengths	6	7	8	9	10	11	12	13	14	Lengths
Metres	pts.	pts.	pts.	pts.	pts.	pts.	pts.	pts.	pts.	Metres
0	595	670	745	820	895	970	1045	1120	1195	0
1	598	673	748	823	898	973	1048	1123	1198	1
2	601	676	751	826	901	976	1051	1126	1201	2
3	604	679	754	829	904	979	1054	1129	1204	3
4	607	682	757	832	907	982	1057	1132	1207	4
5	610	685	760	835	910	985	1060	1135	1210	5
6	613	688	763	838	913	988	1063	1138	1213	6
7	616	691	766	841	916	991	1066	1141	1216	7
8	619	694	769	844	919	994	1069	1144	1219	8
9	622	697	772	847	922	997	1072	1147	1222	9
10	625	700	775	850	925	1000	1075	1150	1225	10
11	628	703	778	853	928	1003	1078	1153	1228	11
12	631	706	781	856	931	1006	1081	1156	1231	12
13	634	709	784	859	934	1009	1084	1159	1234	13
14	637	712	787	862	937	1012	1087	1162	1237	14
15	640	715	790	865	940	1015	1090	1165	1240	15
16	643	718	793	868	943	1018	1093	1168	1243	16
17	646	721	796	871	946	1021	1096	1171	1246	17
18	649	724	799	874	949	1024	1099	1174	1249	18
19	652	727	802	877	952	1027	1102	1177	1252	19
20	655	730	805	880	955	1030	1105	1180	1255	20
21	658	733	808	883	958	1033	1108	1183	1258	21
22	661	736	811	886	961	1036	1111	1186	1261	22
23	664	739	814	889	964	1039	1114	1189	1264	23
24	667	742	817	892	967	1042	1117	1192	1267	24

Ready Reckoner for 25 metre pool

1000 points for   9   Lengths   0   Metres   +/- 3 points per Metre

Lengths	4		5		6		7		8		9		10		11		12	Lengths
Metres	pts.		pts.		pts.		pts.		pts.		pts.		pts.		pts.		pts.	Metres
0	625		700		775		850		925		1000		1075		1150		1225	0
1	628		703		778		853		928		1003		1078		1153		1228	1
2	631		706		781		856		931		1006		1081		1156		1231	2
3	634		709		784		859		934		1009		1084		1159		1234	3
4	637		712		787		862		937		1012		1087		1162		1237	4
5	640		715		790		865		940		1015		1090		1165		1240	5
6	643		718		793		868		943		1018		1093		1168		1243	6
7	646		721		796		871		946		1021		1096		1171		1246	7
8	649		724		799		874		949		1024		1099		1174		1249	8
9	652		727		802		877		952		1027		1102		1177		1252	9
10	655		730		805		880		955		1030		1105		1180		1255	10
11	658		733		808		883		958		1033		1108		1183		1258	11
12	661		736		811		886		961		1036		1111		1186		1261	12
13	664		739		814		889		964		1039		1114		1189		1264	13
14	667		742		817		892		967		1042		1117		1192		1267	14
15	670		745		820		895		970		1045		1120		1195		1270	15
16	673		748		823		898		973		1048		1123		1198		1273	16
17	676		751		826		901		976		1051		1126		1201		1276	17
18	679		754		829		904		979		1054		1129		1204		1279	18
19	682		757		832		907		982		1057		1132		1207		1282	19
20	685		760		835		910		985		1060		1135		1210		1285	20
21	688		763		838		913		988		1063		1138		1213		1288	21
22	691		766		841		916		991		1066		1141		1216		1291	22
23	694		769		844		919		994		1069		1144		1219		1294	23
24	697		772		847		922		997		1072		1147		1222		1297	24

TETRATHLON JUNIOR AND GRASSROOTS SWIMMING

Ready Reckoner for 25 metre pool

1000 points for   7   Lengths   10   Metres   +/- 3 points per Metre

Lengths	3	4	5	6	7	8	9	10	Lengths
Metres	pts.	pts.	pts.	pts.	pts.	pts.	pts.	pts.	Metres
0	670	745	820	895	970	1045	1120	1195	0
1	673	748	823	898	973	1048	1123	1198	1
2	676	751	826	901	976	1051	1126	1201	2
3	679	754	829	904	979	1054	1120	1204	3
4	682	757	832	907	982	1057	1132	1207	4
5	685	760	835	910	985	1060	1135	1210	5
6	688	763	838	913	988	1063	1138	1213	6
7	691	766	841	916	991	1066	1141	1216	7
8	694	769	844	919	994	1069	1144	1219	8
9	697	772	847	922	997	1072	1147	1222	9
10	700	775	850	925	1000	1075	1150	1225	10
11	703	778	853	928	1003	1078	1153	1228	11
12	706	781	856	931	1006	1081	1156	1231	12
13	709	784	859	934	1009	1084	1159	1234	13
14	712	787	862	937	1012	1087	1162	1237	14
15	715	790	865	940	1015	1090	1165	1240	15
16	718	793	868	943	1018	1093	1168	1243	16
17	721	796	871	946	1021	1096	1171	1246	17
18	724	799	874	949	1024	1099	1174	1249	18
19	727	802	877	952	1027	1102	1177	1252	19
20	730	805	880	955	1030	1105	1180	1255	20
21	733	808	883	958	1033	1108	1183	1258	21
22	736	811	886	961	1036	1111	1186	1261	22
23	739	814	889	964	1039	1114	1189	1264	23
24	742	817	892	967	1042	1117	1192	1267	24

TETRATHLON OPEN BOYS RUNNING

1000 points for 10 mins 30 seconds +/- 3 points per second ,

mins	9	10	11	12	13	14	15	16 mins
secs	pts.	pts.	pts.	pts.	pts.	pts.	pts.	secs
0	1270	1090	910	730	550	458	398	338	0
1	1267	1087	907	727	547	457	397	337	1
2	1264	1084	904	724	544	456	396	336	2
3	1261	1081	901	721	541	455	395	335	3
4	1258	1078	898	718	538	454	394	334	4
5	1255	1075	895	715	535	453	393	333	5
6	1252	1072	892	712	532	452	392	332	6
7	1249	1069	889	709	529	451	391	331	7
8	1246	1066	886	706	526	450	390	330	8
9	1243	1063	883	703	523	449	389	329	9
10	1240	1060	880	700	520	448	388	328	10
11	1237	1057	877	697	517	447	387	327	11
12	1234	1054	874	694	514	446	386	326	12
13	1231	1051	871	691	511	445	385	325	13
14	1228	1048	868	688	508	444	384	324	14
15	1225	1045	865	685	505	443	383	323	15
16	1222	1042	862	682	502	442	382	322	16
17	1219	1039	859	679	501	441	381	321	17
18	1216	1036	856	676	500	440	380	320	18
19	1213	1033	853	673	499	439	379	319	19
20	1210	1030	850	670	498	438	378	318	20
21	1207	1027	847	667	497	437	377	317	21
22	1204	1024	844	664	496	436	376	316	22
23	1201	1021	841	661	495	435	375	315	23
24	1198	1018	838	658	494	434	374	314	24
25	1195	1015	835	655	493	433	373	313	25
26	1192	1012	832	652	492	432	372	312	26
27	1189	1009	829	649	491	431	371	311	27
28	1186	1006	826	646	490	430	370	310	28
29	1183	1003	823	643	489	429	369	309	29
30	1180	1000	820	640	488	428	368	308	30
31	1177	997	817	637	487	427	367	307	31
32	1174	994	814	634	486	426	366	306	32
33	1171	991	811	631	485	425	365	305	33
34	1168	988	808	628	484	424	364	304	34
35	1165	985	805	625	483	423	363	303	35
36	1162	982	802	622	482	422	362	302	36
37	1159	979	799	619	481	421	361	301	37
38	1156	976	796	616	480	420	360	300	38
39	1153	973	793	613	479	419	359	299	39
40	1150	970	790	610	478	418	358	298	40
41	1147	967	787	607	477	417	357	297	41
42	1144	964	784	604	476	416	356	296	42
43	1141	961	781	601	475	415	355	295	43
44	1138	958	778	598	474	414	354	294	44
45	1135	955	775	595	473	413	353	293	45
46	1132	952	772	592	472	412	352	292	46
47	1129	949	769	589	471	411	351	291	47
48	1126	946	766	586	470	410	350	290	48
49	1123	943	763	583	469	409	349	289	49
50	1120	940	760	580	468	408	348	288	50
51	1117	937	757	577	467	407	347	287	51
52	1114	934	754	574	466	406	346	286	52
53	1111	931	751	571	465	405	345	285	53
54	1108	928	748	568	464	404	344	284	54
55	1105	925	745	565	463	403	343	283	55
56	1102	922	742	562	462	402	342	282	56
57	1099	919	739	559	461	401	341	281	57
58	1096	916	736	556	460	400	340	280	58
59	1093	913	733	553	459	399	339	279	59

Ready Reckoner for 25 metre pool

1000 points for 5 Lengths 0 Metres +/- 3 points per Metre

Lengths	1	2	3	4	5	6	7	8	9	Lengths
Metres	pts.	pts.	pts.	pts.	pts.	pts.	pts.	pts.	pts.	Metres
0	700	775	850	925	1000	1075	1150	1225	1300	0
1	703	778	853	928	1003	1078	1153	1228	1303	1
2	706	781	856	931	1006	1081	1156	1231	1306	2
3	709	784	859	934	1009	1084	1159	1234	1309	3
4	712	787	862	937	1012	1087	1162	1237	1312	4
5	715	790	865	940	1015	1090	1165	1240	1315	5
6	718	793	868	943	1018	1093	1168	1243	1318	6
7	721	796	871	946	1021	1096	1171	1246	1321	7
8	724	799	874	949	1024	1099	1174	1249	1324	8
9	727	802	877	952	1027	1102	1177	1252	1327	9
10	730	805	880	955	1030	1105	1180	1255	1330	10
11	733	808	883	958	1033	1108	1183	1258	1333	11
12	736	811	886	961	1036	1111	1186	1261	1336	12
13	739	814	889	964	1039	1114	1189	1264	1339	13
14	742	817	892	967	1042	1117	1192	1267	1342	14
15	745	820	895	970	1045	1120	1195	1270	1345	15
16	748	823	898	973	1048	1123	1198	1273	1348	16
17	751	826	901	976	1051	1126	1201	1276	1351	17
18	754	829	904	979	1054	1129	1204	1279	1354	18
19	757	832	907	982	1057	1132	1207	1282	1357	19
20	760	835	910	985	1060	1135	1210	1285	1360	20
21	763	838	913	988	1063	1138	1213	1288	1363	21
22	766	841	916	991	1066	1141	1216	1291	1366	22
23	769	844	919	994	1069	1144	1219	1294	1369	23
24	772	847	922	997	1072	1147	1222	1297	1372	24

TETRATHLON OPEN & INTERMEDIATE GIRLS RUNNING

1000 points for 5 mins 20 seconds +/- 3 points per second

mins	4	5	6	7	8	9 mins
secs	pts.	pts.	pts.	pts.	pts.	pts.	secs
0	1240	1060	880	700	520	340	0
1	1237	1057	877	697	517	337	1
2	1234	1054	874	694	514	334	2
3	1231	1051	871	691	511	331	3
4	1228	1048	868	688	508	328	4
5	1225	1045	865	685	505	325	5
6	1222	1042	862	682	502	322	6
7	1219	1039	859	679	499	319	7
8	1216	1036	856	676	496	316	8
9	1213	1033	853	673	493	313	9
10	1210	1030	850	670	490	310	10
11	1207	1027	847	667	487	307	11
12	1204	1024	844	664	484	304	12
13	1201	1021	841	661	481	301	13
14	1198	1018	838	658	478	298	14
15	1195	1015	835	655	475	295	15
16	1192	1012	832	652	472	292	16
17	1189	1009	829	649	469	289	17
18	1186	1006	826	646	466	286	18
19	1183	1003	823	643	463	283	19
20	1180	1000	820	640	460	280	20
21	1177	997	817	637	457	277	21
22	1174	994	814	634	454	274	22
23	1171	991	811	631	451	271	23
24	1168	988	808	628	448	268	24
25	1165	985	805	625	445	265	25
26	1162	982	802	622	442	262	26
27	1159	979	799	619	439	259	27
28	1156	976	796	616	436	256	28
29	1153	973	793	613	433	253	29
30	1150	970	790	610	430	250	30
31	1147	967	787	607	427	247	31
32	1144	964	784	604	424	244	32
33	1141	961	781	601	421	241	33
34	1138	958	778	598	418	238	34
35	1135	955	775	595	415	235	35
36	1132	952	772	592	412	232	36
37	1129	949	769	589	409	229	37
38	1126	946	766	586	406	226	38
39	1123	943	763	583	403	223	39
40	1120	940	760	580	400	220	40
41	1117	937	757	577	397	217	41
42	1114	934	754	574	394	214	42
43	1111	931	751	571	391	211	43
44	1108	928	748	568	388	208	44
45	1105	925	745	565	385	205	45
46	1102	922	742	562	382	202	46
47	1099	919	739	559	379	199	47
48	1096	916	736	556	376	196	48
49	1093	913	733	553	373	193	49
50	1090	910	730	550	370	190	50
51	1087	907	727	547	367	187	51
52	1084	904	724	544	364	184	52
53	1081	901	721	541	361	181	53
54	1078	898	718	538	358	178	54
55	1075	895	715	535	355	175	55
56	1072	892	712	532	352	172	56
57	1069	889	709	529	349	169	57
58	1066	886	706	526	346	166	58
59	1063	883	703	523	343	163	59

TETRATHLON INTERMEDIATE BOYS RUNNING

1000 points for 7 mins 0 seconds +/- 3 points per second

mins	5	6	7	8	9	10	11	mins
secs	pts.	pts.	pts.	pts.	pts.	pts.	pts.	secs
0	1360	1180	1000	820	640	460	280	0
1	1357	1177	997	817	637	457	277	1
2	1354	1174	994	814	634	454	274	2
3	1351	1171	991	811	631	451	271	3
4	1348	1168	988	808	628	448	268	4
5	1345	1165	985	805	625	445	265	5
6	1342	1162	982	802	622	442	262	6
7	1339	1159	979	799	619	439	259	7
8	1336	1156	976	796	616	436	256	8
9	1333	1153	973	793	613	433	253	9
10	1330	1150	970	790	610	430	250	10
11	1327	1147	967	787	607	427	247	11
12	1324	1144	964	784	604	424	244	12
13	1321	1141	961	781	601	421	241	13
14	1318	1138	958	778	598	418	238	14
15	1315	1135	955	775	595	415	235	15
16	1312	1132	952	772	592	412	232	16
17	1309	1129	949	769	589	409	229	17
18	1306	1126	946	766	586	406	226	18
19	1303	1123	943	763	583	403	223	19
20	1300	1120	940	760	580	400	220	20
21	1297	1117	937	757	577	397	217	21
22	1294	1114	934	754	574	394	214	22
23	1291	1111	931	751	571	391	211	23
24	1288	1108	928	748	568	388	208	24
25	1285	1105	925	745	565	385	205	25
26	1282	1102	922	742	562	382	202	26
27	1279	1099	919	739	559	379	199	27
28	1276	1096	916	736	556	376	196	28
29	1273	1093	913	733	553	373	193	29
30	1270	1090	910	730	550	370	190	30
31	1267	1087	907	727	547	367	187	31
32	1264	1084	904	724	544	364	184	32
33	1261	1081	901	721	541	361	181	33
34	1258	1078	898	718	538	358	178	34
35	1255	1075	895	715	535	355	175	35
36	1252	1072	892	712	532	352	172	36
37	1249	1069	889	709	529	349	169	37
38	1246	1066	886	706	526	346	166	38
39	1243	1063	883	703	523	343	163	39
40	1240	1060	880	700	520	340	160	40
41	1237	1057	877	697	517	337	157	41
42	1234	1054	874	694	514	334	154	42
43	1231	1051	871	691	511	331	151	43
44	1228	1048	868	688	508	328	148	44
45	1225	1045	865	685	505	325	145	45
46	1222	1042	862	682	502	322	142	46
47	1219	1039	859	679	499	319	139	47
48	1216	1036	856	676	496	316	136	48
49	1213	1033	853	673	493	313	133	49
50	1210	1030	850	670	490	310	130	50
51	1207	1027	847	667	487	307	127	51
52	1204	1024	844	664	484	304	124	52
53	1201	1021	841	661	481	301	121	53
54	1198	1018	838	658	478	298	118	54
55	1195	1015	835	655	475	295	115	55
56	1192	1012	832	652	472	292	112	56
57	1189	1009	829	649	469	289	109	57
58	1186	1006	826	646	466	286	106	58
59	1183	1003	823	643	463	283	103	59

TETRATHLON JUNIOR BOYS RUNNING

1000 points for 5 mins 10 seconds +/- 3 points per second

mins	4	5	6	7	8	9	mins
secs	pts.	pts.	pts.	pts.	pts.	pts.	secs
0	1210	1030	850	670	490	310	0
1	1207	1027	847	667	487	307	1
2	1204	1024	844	664	484	304	2
3	1201	1021	841	661	481	301	3
4	1198	1018	838	658	478	298	4
5	1195	1015	835	655	475	295	5
6	1192	1012	832	652	472	292	6
7	1189	1009	829	649	469	289	7
8	1186	1006	826	646	466	286	8
9	1183	1003	823	643	463	283	9
10	1180	1000	820	640	460	280	10
11	1177	997	817	637	457	277	11
12	1174	994	814	634	454	274	12
13	1171	991	811	631	451	271	13
14	1168	988	808	628	448	268	14
15	1165	985	805	625	445	265	15
16	1162	982	802	622	442	262	16
17	1159	979	799	619	439	259	17
18	1156	976	796	616	436	256	18
19	1153	973	793	613	433	253	19
20	1150	970	790	610	430	250	20
21	1147	967	787	607	427	247	21
22	1144	964	784	604	424	244	22
23	1141	961	781	601	421	241	23
24	1138	958	778	598	418	238	24
25	1135	955	775	595	415	235	25
26	1132	952	772	592	412	232	26
27	1129	949	769	589	409	229	27
28	1126	946	766	586	406	226	28
29	1123	943	763	583	403	223	29
30	1120	940	760	580	400	220	30
31	1117	937	757	577	397	217	31
32	1114	934	754	574	394	214	32
33	1111	931	751	571	391	211	33
34	1108	928	748	568	388	208	34
35	1105	925	745	565	385	205	35
36	1102	922	742	562	382	202	36
37	1099	919	739	559	379	199	37
38	1096	916	736	556	376	196	38
39	1093	913	733	553	373	193	39
40	1090	910	730	550	370	190	40
41	1087	907	727	547	367	187	41
42	1084	904	724	544	364	184	42
43	1081	901	721	541	361	181	43
44	1078	898	718	538	358	178	44
45	1075	895	715	535	355	175	45
46	1072	892	712	532	352	172	46
47	1069	889	709	529	349	169	47
48	1066	886	706	526	346	166	48
49	1063	883	703	523	343	163	49
50	1060	880	700	520	340	160	50
51	1057	877	697	517	337	157	51
52	1054	874	694	514	334	154	52
53	1051	871	691	511	331	151	53
54	1048	868	688	508	328	148	54
55	1045	865	685	505	325	145	55
56	1042	862	682	502	322	142	56
57	1039	859	679	499	319	139	57
58	1036	856	676	496	316	136	58
59	1033	853	673	493	313	133	59

TETRATHLON JUNIOR GIRLS RUNNING

mins	4	5	mins	6	40	7	seconds	8	+/- 3 points per second	9	mins
secs	pts.	pts.		pts.		pts.		pts.		pts.	secs
0	1300	1120		940		760		580		400	0
1	1297	1117		937		757		577		397	1
2	1294	1114		934		754		574		394	2
3	1291	1111		931		751		571		391	3
4	1288	1108		928		748		568		388	4
5	1285	1105		925		745		565		385	5
6	1282	1102		922		742		562		382	6
7	1279	1099		919		739		559		379	7
8	1276	1096		916		736		556		376	8
9	1273	1093		913		733		553		373	9
10	1270	1090		910		730		550		370	10
11	1267	1087		907		727		547		367	11
12	1264	1084		904		724		544		364	12
13	1261	1081		901		721		541		361	13
14	1258	1078		898		718		538		358	14
15	1255	1075		895		715		535		355	15
16	1252	1072		892		712		532		352	16
17	1249	1069		889		709		529		349	17
18	1246	1066		886		706		526		346	18
19	1243	1063		883		703		523		343	19
20	1240	1060		880		700		520		340	20
21	1237	1057		877		697		517		337	21
22	1234	1054		874		694		514		334	22
23	1231	1051		871		691		511		331	23
24	1228	1048		868		688		508		328	24
25	1225	1045		865		685		505		325	25
26	1222	1042		862		682		502		322	26
27	1219	1039		859		679		499		319	27
28	1216	1036		856		676		496		316	28
29	1213	1033		853		673		493		313	29
30	1210	1030		850		670		490		310	30
31	1207	1027		847		667		487		307	31
32	1204	1024		844		664		484		304	32
33	1201	1021		841		661		481		301	33
34	1198	1018		838		658		478		298	34
35	1195	1015		835		655		475		295	35
36	1192	1012		832		652		472		292	36
37	1189	1009		829		649		469		289	37
38	1186	1006		826		646		466		286	38
39	1183	1003		823		643		463		283	39
40	1180	1000		820		640		460		280	40
41	1177	997		817		637		457		277	41
42	1174	994		814		634		454		274	42
43	1171	991		811		631		451		271	43
44	1168	988		808		628		448		268	44
45	1165	985		805		625		445		265	45
46	1162	982		802		622		442		262	46
47	1159	979		799		619		439		259	47
48	1156	976		796		616		436		256	48
49	1153	973		793		613		433		253	49
50	1150	970		790		610		430		250	50
51	1147	967		787		607		427		247	51
52	1144	964		784		604		424		244	52
53	1141	961		781		601		421		241	53
54	1138	958		778		598		418		238	54
55	1135	955		775		595		415		235	55
56	1132	952		772		592		412		232	56
57	1129	949		769		589		409		229	57
58	1126	946		766		586		406		226	58
59	1123	943		763		583		403		223	59

TETRATHLON MINIMUS, TADPOLES & GRASSROOTS RUNNING

1000 points for 4 mins 0 seconds +/- 3 points per second

mins	2	3	4	5	6	7	8	mins
secs	pts.	pts.	pts.	pts.	pts.	pts.	pts.	secs
0	1360	1180	1000	820	640	460	280	0
1	1357	1177	997	817	637	457	277	1
2	1354	1174	994	814	634	454	274	2
3	1351	1171	991	811	631	451	271	3
4	1348	1168	988	808	628	448	268	4
5	1345	1165	985	805	625	445	265	5
6	1342	1162	982	802	622	442	262	6
7	1339	1159	979	799	619	439	259	7
8	1336	1156	976	796	616	436	256	8
9	1333	1153	973	793	613	433	253	9
10	1330	1150	970	790	610	430	250	10
11	1327	1147	967	787	607	427	247	11
12	1324	1144	964	784	604	424	244	12
13	1321	1141	961	781	601	421	241	13
14	1318	1138	958	778	598	418	238	14
15	1315	1135	955	775	595	415	235	15
16	1312	1132	952	772	592	412	232	16
17	1309	1129	949	769	589	409	229	17
18	1306	1126	946	766	586	406	226	18
19	1303	1123	943	763	583	403	223	19
20	1300	1120	940	760	580	400	220	20
21	1297	1117	937	757	577	397	217	21
22	1294	1114	934	754	574	394	214	22
23	1291	1111	931	751	571	391	211	23
24	1288	1108	928	748	568	388	208	24
25	1285	1105	925	745	565	385	205	25
26	1282	1102	922	742	562	382	202	26
27	1279	1099	919	739	559	379	199	27
28	1276	1096	916	736	556	376	196	28
29	1273	1093	913	733	553	373	193	29
30	1270	1090	910	730	550	370	190	30
31	1267	1087	907	727	547	367	187	31
32	1264	1084	904	724	544	364	184	32
33	1261	1081	901	721	541	361	181	33
34	1258	1078	898	718	538	358	178	34
35	1255	1075	895	715	535	355	175	35
36	1252	1072	892	712	532	352	172	36
37	1249	1069	889	709	529	349	169	37
38	1246	1066	886	706	526	346	166	38
39	1243	1063	883	703	523	343	163	39
40	1240	1060	880	700	520	340	160	40
41	1237	1057	877	697	517	337	157	41
42	1234	1054	874	694	514	334	154	42
43	1231	1051	871	691	511	331	151	43
44	1228	1048	868	688	508	328	148	44
45	1225	1045	865	685	505	325	145	45
46	1222	1042	862	682	502	322	142	46
47	1219	1039	859	679	499	319	139	47
48	1216	1036	856	676	496	316	136	48
49	1213	1033	853	673	493	313	133	49
50	1210	1030	850	670	490	310	130	50
51	1207	1027	847	667	487	307	127	51
52	1204	1024	844	664	484	304	124	52
53	1201	1021	841	661	481	301	121	53
54	1198	1018	838	658	478	298	118	54
55	1195	1015	835	655	475	295	115	55
56	1192	1012	832	652	472	292	112	56
57	1189	1009	829	649	469	289	109	57
58	1186	1006	826	646	466	286	106	58
59	1183	1003	823	643	463	283	103	59

TETRATHLON BEANIES RUNNING

1000 points for		2 mins			0 seconds		+/- 3 points per second	
mins		1	2	3	4		5	mins
secs	pts.		pts.	pts.	pts.		pts.	secs
0	1180	1000	820	640	460			0
1	1177	997	817	637	457			1
2	1174	994	814	634	454			2
3	1171	991	811	631	451			3
4	1168	988	808	628	448			4
5	1165	985	805	625	445			5
6	1162	982	802	622	442			6
7	1159	979	799	619	439			7
8	1156	976	796	616	436			8
9	1153	973	793	613	433			9
10	1150	970	790	610	430			10
11	1147	967	787	607	427			11
12	1144	964	784	604	424			12
13	1141	961	781	601	421			13
14	1138	958	778	598	418			14
15	1135	955	775	595	415			15
16	1132	952	772	592	412			16
17	1129	949	769	589	409			17
18	1126	946	766	586	406			18
19	1123	943	763	583	403			19
20	1120	940	760	580	400			20
21	1117	937	757	577	397			21
22	1114	934	754	574	394			22
23	1111	931	751	571	391			23
24	1108	928	748	568	388			24
25	1105	925	745	565	385			25
26	1102	922	742	562	382			26
27	1099	919	739	559	379			27
28	1096	916	736	556	376			28
29	1093	913	733	553	373			29
30	1090	910	730	550	370			30
31	1087	907	727	547	367			31
32	1084	904	724	544	364			32
33	1081	901	721	541	361			33
34	1078	898	718	538	358			34
35	1075	895	715	535	355			35
36	1072	892	712	532	352			36
37	1069	889	709	529	349			37
38	1066	886	706	526	346			38
39	1063	883	703	523	343			39
40	1060	880	700	520	340			40
41	1057	877	697	517	337			41
42	1054	874	694	514	334			42
43	1051	871	691	511	331			43
44	1048	868	688	508	328			44
45	1045	865	685	505	325			45
46	1042	862	682	502	322			46
47	1039	859	679	499	319			47
48	1036	856	676	496	316			48
49	1033	853	673	493	313			49
50	1030	850	670	490	310			50
51	1027	847	667	487	307			51
52	1024	844	664	484	304			52
53	1021	841	661	481	301			53
54	1018	838	658	478	298			54
55	1015	835	655	475	295			55
56	1012	832	652	472	292			56
57	1009	829	649	469	289			57
58	1006	826	646	466	286			58
59	1003	823	643	463	283			59

APPENDIX B - THE LAW AS IT RELATES TO AIR WEAPONS

ENGLAND AND WALES

1.   AIR WEAPONS AND THE LAW

a.   It is an offence for a person in possession of an air weapon to fail to take reasonable precautions to prevent someone under the age of 18 from gaining unauthorised access to it. A defence is provided where a person can show that they had reasonable grounds for believing the other person to be aged 18 or over. The maximum penalty for someone convicted of this new offence is £1,000.

b.   It is an offence for a person under the age of 18 to purchase or hire an air weapon or ammunition for an air weapon.

c.   It is an offence to sell, let on hire or make a gift of an air weapon or ammunition for an air weapon to a person under the age of 18.

d.   It is an offence for anyone under the age of 18 to have with them an air weapon or ammunition for an air weapon unless:

- ▸ They are under the supervision of a person aged 21 or over;

- ▸ They are shooting as a member of an approved target shooting club;

- ▸ They are shooting at a shooting gallery and the only firearms being used are either air weapons or miniature rifles not exceeding .23 inch calibre;

- ▸ The person is 14 years old or above and is on private premises with the consent of the occupier.

e.   It is an offence to part with possession of an air weapon, or ammunition for an air weapon, to a person under the age of 18 except under the special circumstances mentioned immediately above.

f.   It is an offence for any person shooting on private land, regardless of age, to use an air weapon for firing a pellet beyond the boundaries of the premises.

g.   It is an offence for a supervising adult to allow a person under the age of 18 to use an air weapon for firing a pellet beyond the boundaries of premises.

h.   It is an offence for any person to have an air weapon in a public place without a reasonable excuse. While there is no statutory definition of a reasonable excuse, it might include carrying a weapon to and from a shooting club, or taking a new weapon home from a dealer. However, it is ultimately for the courts to decide what a reasonable excuse is.

i.   It is an offence to trespass with an air weapon, whether in a building or on land.

j.   It is an offence to have an air weapon if you are prohibited from possessing a firearm. Anyone who has been sentenced to a custodial sentence of between three months and three years is prohibited from possessing an air weapon or other firearm or ammunition for five years from the date of their release. Anyone who has been sentenced to three years or more is prohibited for life.

k.   It is an offence to fire an air weapon without lawful authority or excuse within 50 feet (15 metres) of the centre of a public road in such a way as to cause a road user to be injured, interrupted or endangered.

l.   It is an offence to intentionally or recklessly kill certain wild animals and birds. When shooting live quarry, it is your responsibility to make sure that you only do so legally.

m.   It is an offence to knowingly cause a pet animal to suffer unnecessarily, which could be committed by shooting at a pet animal.

n.   It is an offence to have an air weapon with intent to damage or to destroy property. It is also an offence to have air weapons and be reckless as to whether property would be damaged or destroyed.

o.   It is an offence to have an air weapon with intent to end

2.   SAFE HANDLING

a.   Always treat an air weapon as though it were loaded.

b.   Always point an air weapon in a safe direction, preferably at the ground, and never at another person.

c.   Never load an air weapon until you are ready to fire it.

d.   Never fire an air weapon unless you are certain that the shot will be safe. This means checking that there is nothing and no one nearby who might be endangered by the shot and ensuring that there is a suitable backstop or pellet catcher to prevent ricochets.

e.   Never rely on a safety catch to make an air weapon safe. Such devices can fail.

f.   Never put a loaded air weapon down. Always safely discharge or unload and uncock it first.

g.   Never store a loaded air weapon.

h.   Air weapons should be stored out of sight and separately from pellets.

i.   Air weapons should be covered, for example in a gun slip, when being transported.

j.   Air weapons must not be stored where unauthorised people, particularly young people under the age of 18, might gain access to them. For example, use a lockable cupboard and keep the keys secure. Air weapons should be stored inside a house rather than in an outbuilding, such as a garden shed.

k.   Consider ways of rendering a stored air weapon incapable of being fired.

3.   SAFE STORAGE

a.   In many cases, it will be sufficient to store your air weapon in an existing, suitably robust, lockable cupboard – keeping the keys separate and secure.

b.   Alternatively, you could use a lock or locking device by which your air weapon can be attached to the fabric of a building, or to a fixed feature. Or you could use a security cord, lockable chain or similar device attached to a point of anchorage within the building.

c.   Even where children are very young, or are not normally present, it is preferable to use some form of security cord or similar device rather than simply storing your air weapon up high and out of reach.

d.   Anyone who already holds other firearms could use their existing gun cabinet for their air weapon provided this does not compromise security.

e.   Air weapons should be stored within the occupied part of a building and not in an outbuilding, such as a garage or shed.

f.   If you keep a number of air weapons, you might find it useful to consider some of the security measures suggested for licensed firearms. This information can be found in the Firearms Security Handbook 2005, available on the Home Office website.

g. When using your air weapon, the best advice is to keep it under close supervision at all times and to never leave it unattended.

h. Where you have no option but to put your air weapon down for short periods, unload it and gather up all the ammunition.

Steps should then be taken to prevent anyone under the age of 18 from gaining unauthorised access to It. Where practicable, this could include attaching it to a fixed object using a security cord or similar device, or locking it out of sight in a car.

Northern Ireland

The Firearms (NI) Order 2004 states that, unless exempted, a firearm certificate is required for the purchase and possession of firearms and ammunition in Northern Ireland.

This makes it an offence for any person to purchase, acquire or have in their possession, a firearm or ammunition without holding a valid firearm certificate. One firearm certificate is issued to an individual to licence all approved firearms in their possession.

Airguns and CO_2 guns having a discharge kinetic energy in excess of one (1) Joule (0.737 ft lbs) require to be held on a firearm certificate. Air guns must still meet The Pony Club requirements of having a discharge kinetic energy under 6 foot lbs (rule 53b). For airguns below the one (1) Joule limit the following restrictions are in place:

- Under Paragraph 9 of Schedule 1 of the Firearms (NI) Order 2004, persons under the age of 18 cannot possess such firearms, unless they have attained the age of 14 years or are under the direct supervision of a person of 21 years or over.
- Persons not holding a firearms certificate cannot purchase such firearms, unless they have attained the age of 17 years.
- Ammunition for an airgun can be purchased and possessed without holding a firearm certificate.

The control of firearms in Northern Ireland is exercised by the Chief Constable. Before a person can be authorised to hold a firearm certificate, the Chief Constable must be satisfied that the applicant:

- Is not prohibited by law from possessing a firearm, is not of intemperate habits or unsound mind and is not, for any reason, unfit to be entrusted with a firearm.
- Has good reason for purchasing, acquiring or having in their possession the firearm or ammunition in respect of which the application is made.

- ▸ Can be permitted to have that firearm or ammunition in their possession without danger to public safety or to the peace.

Scotland

For the purposes of the Air Weapons and Licensing Scotland Act 2015 –

- ▸ any current member participating in Tetrathlon activities in Scotland is deemed to be a member of the Scottish Tetrathlon Air Pistol Club, and

- ▸ any parent/guardian of a current member participating in Tetrathlon activities in Scotland is deemed to be a member of the Scottish Tetrathlon Air Pistol Club.

Under the Air Weapons and Licensing (Scotland) Act 2015 it is a legal requirement for a person to have an Air Weapons Certificate to use, possess, purchase or acquire an Air Weapon over 1 joule of muzzle energy in Scotland, unless they are exempt under the legislation.

To apply for a licence for an air weapon you must complete an AWL1 form which can be downloaded from the Police Scotland website -

https://www.scotland.police.uk/about-us/what-we-do/firearms-and-explosives-licensing/air-weapons/

APPENDIX C - ARENA JUMPING RULES

A Show Jumping course of twelve fences to include a double and a treble. If possible, a slip rail and gate will be included (to be Judged as for cross country). Alternatively, if a gate is unavailable a stay in box can be used, in which the horse/pony must be stationary within the box for 4 seconds.

Maximum height of fences will be as per Rule 28.

Scoring (Maximum score 1400):

▸ **Knockdown**
   30 penalties
▸ **First Refusal**
   60 penalties
▸ **Second Refusal at the same fence**
   100 penalties
▸ **Third Refusal at the same fence**
   Retirement and 500 penalties, each fence not jumped after retirement is 50 penalties
▸ **L Fence (optional)**
   70 penalties
▸ **Fall**
   90 penalties
▸ **2 falls**
   Retirement
▸ **Fall of horse**
   Retirement
▸ **Each fence not jumped after retirement**
   50 penalties
▸ **Error of Course not rectified**
   Retirement
▸ **Failure to stay in box for 4 seconds**
   20 penalties

Timing:

▸ **Speed**
   PC80 - 325 mpm
   PC90/PC100 - 375mpm
   30 seconds for gate, Slip rail or stay in box if included
▸ **Each commenced second over the time allowed**
   2 penalties
▸ **75 Secs over the time allowed**
   Retirement

These are suggested timings and maybe adjusted should the Judge consider it to be an appropriate action.

The stay in the box – horse/pony must be within the box otherwise they get 20 penalties

No stop watches allowed.

The Course:

Safety Cups are now compulsory for all Pony Club Jumping Competitions. To be use on the back rails of spread fences and middle and back rails of triple bars. This will also include practice fences in the collecting ring. These cups must be in use at all times and must NOT be removed from the wing stands.

Practice Fences:

Safety Cups must be used on the back rails of spread fences. These cups must be in use at all times and must NOT be removed from the wing stands.

APPENDIX D - WINTER TRIATHLON RULES

One Qualifying competition in each Area.

All competitors must be Pony Club Members and have qualified at one of the qualifying Triathlons competitions as shown on The Pony Club website.

Each area will have the two highest placed members of the area qualify. If competitors from out of area are placed 1st or 2nd and not already qualified, they will also qualify. In the case of 1st or 2nd placed competitors having already qualified, the place will be passed onto the next highest placed competitor.

Each Area can declare one Open Team, two Junior and two Minimus teams which have four competitors in, the team can be any mix of boys and girls. Declarations must be submitted in writing to the Secretary by the Area Tetrathlon Co–ordinator or designated person by midday on 21st March 2024.

It is the responsibility of the competitors to ensure that they inform the Organiser before the start of a competition if they have already qualified previously so if they win the qualifying place will be given to the next highest placed competitor.

Minimus aged 11 or under on 1st Jan of the current calendar year (Must be aged 8 on day of competition)

Junior aged 14 or under on 1st Jan of the current calendar year Open aged 25 or under on 1st Jan of the current calendar year

Directly funded Pentathlon GB athletes (currently Podium Potential and Podium Level) may compete HC at the discretion of the Tetrathlon Chairman.

Class	Run	Swim	Shoot
Minimus	1000m	2 minutes	7m Turning targets (Can use 2 hands)
Junior	1500m	3 minutes	7m Turning targets
Open (Inc. Intermediates) GIRLS	1500m	3 minutes	10m Turning targets

Open (Inc. Intermediates) BOYS	3000m	4 minutes	10m Turning targets

Rosettes will be 1st-10th Individuals and 1st-10th Teams in all classes.

APPENDIX E – STEPPINGSTONE MINIMUS REGIONAL TEAM COMPETITION

TO BE HELD AT THE TETRATHLON CHAMPIONSHIPS

ELIGIBILITY

Competitors must not have competed at Junior level or above at Regional or Area competitions.

Minimus Regional Team Competition - Open to Members aged 11 and under (on 1st January of the current calendar year). Teams of four or five and can be any mix of boys or girls. If a team consists of five, then its score is the sum of the best four performances overall.

Minimus Individual Competition - Open to Minimus Regional Team competitors. The scores for all competitors automatically count for this competition. Boys and Girls will be split.

No horse or pony may complete more than 3 Show Jumping rounds.

ENTRIES

All competitors must be a minimum of 8 years old on the day of the competition. Entries via Regional Team Managers who must certify that all members are competent to shoot prior to the commencement of the shooting phase.

Priority entries will be given to 2 teams per region. Numbers will be limited.

Entries to be completed online as per The Pony Club Championships

COMPETITION FORMAT

Friday

- Swim – 2 Minutes
- Shoot – 7 Metres, turning targets, two handed
- Run – 1000m

Saturday

- Ride – Show Jumping course with a slip rail and halt box, to be run in accordance with Arena Jumping rules (Appendix C) - Height 80cm.

SCORING/AWARDS

In accordance with current Tetrathlon Rules.

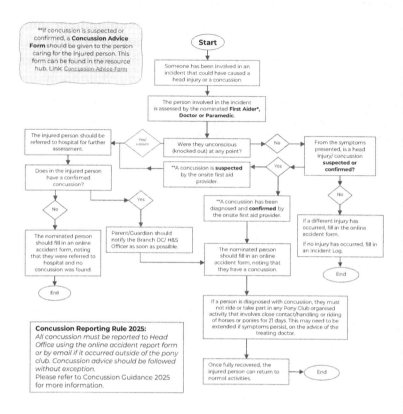

If concussion is suspected or confirmed, a **Concussion Advice Form should be given to the person caring for the Injured person. This form can be found in the resource hub. Link: Concussion-Advice-Form

Start

Someone has been involved in an incident that could have caused a head injury or a concussion.

The person involved in the incident is assessed by the nominated **First Aider*, Doctor or Paramedic.**

Were they unconscious (knocked out) at any point?

The injured person should be referred to hospital for further assessment.

From the symptoms presented, is a head injury/ concussion **suspected or confirmed?**

A concussion is **suspected by the onsite first aid provider.

Does in the injured person have a confirmed concussion?

A concussion has been diagnosed and **confirmed by the onsite first aid provider.

If a different injury has occurred, fill in the online accident form.

If no injury has occurred, fill in an incident Log.

End

The nominated person should fill in an online accident form, noting that they were referred to hospital and no concussion was found.

Parent/Guardian should notify the Branch DC/ H&S Officer as soon as possible.

The nominated person should fill in an online accident form, noting that they have a concussion.

End

If a person is diagnosed with concussion, they must not ride or take part in any Pony Club organised activity that involves close contact/handling or riding of horses or ponies for 21 days. This may need to be extended if symptoms persist, on the advice of the treating doctor.

Once fully recovered, the injured person can return to normal activities.

End

Concussion Reporting Rule 2025:
All concussion must be reported to Head Office using the online accident report form or by email if it occurred outside of the pony club. Concussion advice should be followed without exception.
Please refer to Concussion Guidance 2025 for more information.

* If concussion is diagnosed by a first aider, this diagnosis can only be overruled by a doctor and letter evidence will be required.

If you need any advice or support, please contact the Safety Team Safety@PCUK.org

Printed in Great Britain
by Amazon